D0447779

Kahuna Healing

Cover art by *Jane A. Evans*

Kahuna Healing

Holistic health and healing practices of Polynesia

By *Serge King*

*This publication made possible with
the assistance of the Kern Foundation*

The Theosophical Publishing House
Wheaton, Ill. U.S.A.
Madras, India/London, England

© Copyright by Serge King, 1983
A Quest original. First edition 1983.
Third Printing, 1986.
All rights reserved.
No part of this book may be reproduced in any manner
without written permission except for quotations
embodied in critical articles or reviews.
For additional information write to:
The Theosophical Publishing House,
306 West Geneva Road,
Wheaton, Illinois 60187.
Published by The Theosophical Publishing House,
a department of the Theosophical Society in America.

Library of Congress Cataloging in Publication Data

King, Serge.
    Kahuna healing.
    "A Quest original"—T.p. verso
    Bibliography: p.
    Includes index.
    1. Mental healing.   2. Healing—Hawaii.
    3. Hawaiians—Medicine   I. Title
RZ401.K54   1983   615.8'51   82-42704
ISBN 0-8356-0572-8 (pbk.)

Printed in the United States of America

Table of Contents

This book is dedicated to *Harry L. King*, my father and my first Huna teacher;

to *O.*, who kept Huna alive in me as I grew up;

to *M'Bala*, who taught me so much about psychic energy;

and especially to *Wana Kahili*, whose deep knowledge of Huna philosophy and traditions made this presentation possible.

Prologue

"Sandstorm!" Camels groaned, horses whinnied, and the small group of men rushed to protect the heads of their animals from the biting dust before covering their own faces with woolen scarves. In typical Gobi fashion, the storm had come upon them almost without warning. The men coughed and cursed in Mongolian and English as they crowded together and stumbled forward. One of the guides had noticed some mounds of sand off to their left before the storm hit, and it was toward these that he led the party in hopes of finding some small protection from the wind and sand. Minutes later he bumped into the remains of a mud brick wall, left from one of the ancient village ruins that still dot that desert. "Shelter! Shelter here!" he shouted. His voice was muffled by scarf and wind, but the word was heard and passed along. Men and animals struggled ahead to locate themselves in the protective nooks and crannies of broken walls and piles of rubble. Apparently, chance had smiled upon them.

One of the men, the youngest of the foreigners on this scientific-cum-political expedition, found shelter at the juncture of two walls some distance from the others. There he settled down his pack horse and crouched next to the animal to wait out the storm. The expedition of which he was a part was one of many sent out by England in the early part of the twentieth century when Asia was still a pawn in the power struggles between the British, Russian and Chinese empires. The young man was musing on this when suddenly the ground in front of his feet seemed to crumble away, leaving a gaping hole before him. In the hazy glow of sand-screened sunlight he saw steps leading down into the darkness. He must be on the roof of an old building, he thought, and his short trek across it had weakened the supports. Highly curious and oblivious to any danger, he left his horse and descended the stairs.

Enough light filtered through the hole to give him a dim view of his surroundings, and what he saw made him gasp with surprise. He stood in a room some thirty or forty feet long and about fifteen feet wide. Along the walls on either side were what appeared to be painted frescoes, but there was not enough light to make out the subject matter. He moved further into the room and was able to see a table or stand at the far end. On reaching it he saw that it looked more like a stone altar. Lying in the center of the altar was a piece of jewelry, a bracelet. As he picked it up he heard a noise behind him and he whirled around. Sand was pouring into the opening, threatening to bury him alive. Stuffing the bracelet into a pocket, he dashed back and crawled out. His horse was gone, and the storm was becoming worse. All he could do was to huddle in his corner and wait it out.

At last the storm spent itself. The young man, almost

entirely covered with sand, pushed away the cloth that covered his head and squinted out on a different world. The sun beat down through clear air and there was no trace of the opening through which he had crawled earlier. Sand blanketed everything, even the pieces of walls that had served for shelter. Then he heard voices. "Harry! Harry, where are you?" "Right here," he shouted, and dug himself out of his gritty nest. His horse had been found by the others and they were much relieved to find him intact. No one was interested in his story about a room with frescoes and an altar. They were too anxious to cross this stretch of sand and move on to the steppes. After getting some good-natured kidding about sunstroke, he said no more about his adventure, and the expedition went on its way.

Some months later, Harry was back in London, reporting to his superior in the government bureau for which he worked. Near the end of his recital of his part in the Gobi expedition, he reached into his pocket and pulled out the bracelet. "What do you think of this?" he asked, laying it on the man's desk. "Looks almost like a map of the solar system, doesn't it?" Harry expected mild curiosity, perhaps some admiration, but the man behind the desk looked thunderstruck. Gingerly, he picked up the bracelet and examined it carefully. In its center was a yellow stone, like topaz, and arranged around it at random on concentric golden rings were other, smaller stones, exactly nine. The man looked at Harry piercingly and said, "Where did you get this?" Harry told him the story of the storm and the room he had stumbled into. "May I keep this overnight?" the man asked. "I assure you it will be safe." Though surprised, Harry agreed.

And the next day was the beginning of the strangest

of all Harry's many adventures. Over the following months he was introduced to a group of people who did not believe in chance, and for whom the finding of that bracelet had special meaning. Eventually, he was introduced as well to teachings that, for him, presented an entirely new way of looking at and dealing with reality. And finally, he was adopted/initiated into that group which he always called *The Organization*.

* * *

The young man in the above tale was Harry Leland Loring King, my father, and that is the way he told the story to me. Through him I, too, became associated with The Organization, though I call it by another name. I feel that the knowledge I have gained from this affiliation is so important to health and happiness on both an individual and worldwide scale that I want to share it with you in a form that can make it a living reality in your daily life.

But first I would like to give you some background on myself and the group. Some of you may find what I am going to say difficult to believe, and if you want to take it with a pound of salt, that's all right with me. The real meat of the book begins with Chapter 2, and you can skip right to that if you want. Others, however, may gain some benefit from the realization that there are views of the world and things going on in life that are quite different from what most of us here in the West are brought up to believe.

My first remembrance of anything having to do with the group of which I speak was at the age of seven, when my father read me a letter from a man he said was "watching over my development." I never met that man, but about that time I began to cultivate an intense interest in astronomy that has never abated. From my father I gained a deep love of science and of nature, and I learned many practical lessons in the power of the mind. When I was fourteen, my father initiated me into the group and said that I would be contacted by other teachers as time went on. Then my training began in earnest. Unfortunately, I had only three more years of my father's help before he passed on. The year after his death, while working my way through college, I was contacted by a man from the group who said that for awhile I would be receiving further tutoring through my dreams. At the time I was more interested in physical survival, so I didn't give it much importance. Instead of going on to college for a second year, I joined the Marine Corps and moved to California. After a few months I was contacted by someone else from the group and we met on a fairly regular basis during my whole enlistment. Among other things, I was led into a study of archeology and techniques for looking into the distant past. Just before my military term was up I was ordained as a kahuna of the Order of Kane, about which I'll have more to say later. For the next five years my "extracurricular" studies centered on anthropology, philosophy and religion.

By 1964 I had a family, and I was hired by an American Voluntary Agency to manage relief and development programs in West Africa. There I was contacted by an African member of the group, and with his help I experienced some of the most adventurous years of my life. In Africa I was deeply involved in the techniques of social change and the nature of the life force, particularly as it applies to healing. While working with villagers and government bureaucrats to bring about socioeconomic development I began to see how ineffective most orthodox approaches are in inducing lasting change of any kind. The orthodox way—and this applies to medicine, psychotherapy and education as well as to socioeconomics—is to establish a nice, neat, logical and inflexible method of operation and apply it like law.

This was brought out beautifully in an experience I observed at a meeting between Peace Corps workers and a local government office for community development. The Peace Corpsmen were very upset with the way the local government was handling the development program because it just wasn't working in the field. In other words, the method was not resulting in the desired changes, and the Corpsmen's view was that it didn't take into account what the villagers felt. A spokesman for the government got very angry and said, "There is nothing wrong with the method. It has been designed after a great deal of thought and is perfectly suited to the situation. There is nothing at all wrong with the method. It is the people who have to be changed!" He could have been speaking for the orthodox of every time and place.

But a system like that doesn't work very well for very long, mainly because people are continually changing. It may sound like a paradox at first, but a rigid system imposed from outside actually assumes that people don't change, and that there is less variety in their needs than there really is. By working directly with people's felt needs in the context of their own situations, I was able to come up with a flexible approach to development that was highly successful. I accomplished things that the local government, the U.S. government, and occasionally the Peace Corps and even the villagers at first thought would be impossible. And I did it with meager means and a few simple, basic concepts. What I have found in my years of individual training is that the same basics apply to personal development as to social and economic development.

Concerning healing, I had the privilege while in Africa of establishing a close rapport with several traditional healers who really knew their art. They taught me some fascinating things about what modern researchers are calling bioenergy fields and currents, and also about the relations between mind and body, and body and environment. I learned that it is possible for anyone to become aware of the source of emotional energy, to increase it, to direct it and to use it for healing himself or someone else. What impressed me most was the knowledge that emotions can heal as well as hurt. I started by using this idea on my own family, then taught them how to do it for themselves. Now we teach others.

On returning to the United States in 1971 I made contact with a man I'll call WK, whom I had met briefly on a previous trip. WK is a Hawaiian kahuna, and what he taught me over the next three years has profoundly changed my life and has enabled me to help many others make lasting improvements in every aspect of their own lives. The subjects were simple enough: love, imagination, beliefs and the nature of success. But his understanding of them was unlike anything ordinarily taught to people in this society. I began to see that his view was reflected in my own experience, and furthermore, that it allowed me to change my experience. I realized that here was something that had to be shared. The way I wanted to do it, however, caused a lively discussion. For various reasons, the kahunas of my order have for a long time carried out their work in a private manner, well out of the public eye. The notion I had was unusual, but it was finally agreed that I should found a new order for the purpose of publicly teaching the Huna knowledge. The result was the Order of Huna International, founded in 1973 and chartered by the State of California as a nonprofit, nonsectarian religious order.

However, Huna—the usual name given to kahuna knowledge—is not a religion. It is a philosophy of achievement that can be applied in any context, whether religious, scientific, social or personal. Even the members of Huna International do not have to give up their traditional faith to join, and that includes the kahunas. We have Huna Christians, Huna Jews, Huna Buddhists, Huna Muslims and so on, all of whom find that Huna enhances their appreciation of their own background. No matter what religion you belong to, you are affected by gravity. Huna knowledge is that basic. The only reason people join the order is to share in a mutually cooperative and beneficial venture, for we are making this knowledge available to everyone. Our motto is taken from an ancient cry that Hawaiian kahunas made from an oracle tower: *Let That Which Is Unknown Become Known!*

You may be asking yourself by now, "What is this word *Huna* and what is a kahuna?" *Huna* is a Hawaiian word meaning "that which is hidden, or not obvious." Sometimes we call it the Hidden Knowledge, or the Secret Reality. The idea is not that anyone purposely hid it away, but only that it is usually hard to see. The term kahuna can be translated as "a transmitter of the secret," and it was originally intended to be used for those who belonged to an order which practiced and taught the knowledge. In modern Hawaii, however, the word is used for everything from a Western priest or minister, to ordinary psychics and healers, and to charlatans preying on the gullible. We use it here with its original meaning.

Prologue

Among those people who are familiar with Huna at the present time, most are only acquainted with the works of Max Freedom Long on the subject. Max Long was a student of psychology, religion and psychic science who did some brilliant work in uncovering much of the Huna knowledge that is encoded in the Hawaiian language. The relatively few errors and distortions that crept into his early work are understandable, since he never had an opportunity to discuss his findings with a kahuna. At the time he lived in Hawaii, in the early part of this century, it was against the law to be or even claim to be a kahuna, and this was so until fairly recently. It is amazing that Long was able to do as much as he did with only stories, superstitions and distorted knowledge to go by. Fortunately, he had the kind of mind that was excellent at making correlations with knowledge from other fields and cultures, and he was able to see through most of the distortion.

To stretch your mind a little further, I'd like to give you some of the history of Huna philosophy. It has been said that history is more a reflection of the present than of the past, because historians tend to write about the past in terms of what the present generation is willing to accept. What people can't accept won't be written, or at least not published. As society changes, so do the history books. A minor example is black history in the United States. Before the civil rights movement, black history was almost nonexistent. Nothing was being taught in the schools, no one was studying it, and for all practical purposes there wasn't any such thing in the minds of most people, even blacks. Now it turns out that there were a great many heroic and important black Americans, and the history books are being rewritten, but only because society is now willing to look in that direction.

Much that is written as history is little more than educated guesswork, with the historian playing the role of a time-traveling detective with only spotty clues to guide him. The further back you go in the past, the spottier the clues. It is helpful when there are written records to go by, such as the hieroglyphics in Egypt, but many peoples have oral histories that trace their civilizations much farther back than modern historians are willing to admit is possible. Such histories are usually called myths or legends, with the implication that they probably aren't true.

The history I am about to recount is partly oral and partly recorded. But the recorded part is not in writing as you might understand it. You could be surprised to learn that there are some people who can "read" string figures and carved designs as easily as you read this page. At any rate, this is the history of a philosophy as told to me by WK. If it is unacceptable to you as fact, think of it as a tradition. It won't affect your ability to use the Huna knowledge.

* * * * * *

"At some point in time, long before the rise of Atlantis, a race of men came to this solar system from a group of stars now known as the Pleiades. Some landed on the Earth and others on another planet that no longer exists. At that time the Earth was closer to the sun and the length of the year was exactly 360 days. The men who came from the stars fled catastrophe, and on Earth they intended to find peace. It was a long time in coming, however, because they found other men there already, remnants from a previous civilization that had fallen apart. They also found intelligent dinosaurs, and many battles for territorial control ensued.

"At last most of the starmen settled on a continent in the Pacific known today in legend as Mu. They called themselves the People of Mu, but others called them Manahuna or Menehune, 'the people of the secret power,' because of their advanced technology and psychic powers. They were a small people, pygmy-like by modern standards, and very industrious. Their knowledge was Huna, a fundamental philosophy for successful living. Once they felt securely established, they began to teach this knowledge to the men of Earth. Because many different languages were spoken and because their own was partly telepathic and difficult to learn, the teachers of Mu created a new language that was simple to learn. This language was structured to contain the Huna knowledge within it in a way that would ensure its survival for as long as the language remained in use. Today we know this language as Polynesian, and traces of it are found all over the world.

"Men came to the continent of Mu to learn, and Mu also sent missions of teachers to other parts of the world to set up schools of various types. A fair amount of intermarriage took place between the Mu people and their neighbors, resulting in children who carried on the genetic abilities and memories of their star-born parents.

"Gradually, those who studied with the Mu became organized into three different orders, each one practicing the Huna knowledge with a slightly different emphasis. Using English terms, they could be called the Intuitionists, the Intellectuals and the Emotionals.

"Generally speaking, the Intuitionists developed into what we would call mystics, metaphysicians and psychologists or psychotherapists. The Intellectuals became the equivalent of scientists, technicians and engineers. The Emotionals were more concerned with political, economic and athletic activities. All three made use of trained psychic abilities in their work, and each group taught and practiced various forms of physical healing.

"Now it is a basic part of Huna philosophy that every human being has psychic abilities. The orders trained people in their conscious and disciplined use. Nevertheless, there were people on Earth before the arrival of the Mu who could use these powers at will, and there remain people today unconnected with the orders who can use them in the same way.

"For many centuries things were going well on Earth and a world civilization was in the making when the Mu made a fatal mistake. For quite awhile they had maintained contact with their brethren who had settled on the other planet in the solar system, but eventually they turned all their attention on Earth and left the others to themselves. Then there came a time when desperate calls for help came from the sister planet. The people there were on the verge of destroying themselves and quick intervention was needed. Unfortunately, the Earth Mu had grown complacent and didn't want anything to disturb their peace, so they closed their ears to the pleas and tried to pretend it didn't concern them. In this they acted contrary to their own philosophy.

"With nothing to stop them, the people of the other planet created more and more terrible weapons of destruction to use against each other until the final, awful moment came. They reached a point where they blew their whole planet apart in a mighty cataclysm that rocked the solar system. The complete disappearance of an entire planet caused an immense imbalance, which the forces of nature sought to correct. In so doing, the orbits of the remaining planets were disrupted and the effect on Earth was devastating. Our planet was tumbled into a new orbit a little further from the sun, and the stress of the change caused intense volcanic and earthquake activity. Old lands sank beneath the seas in some places and new lands rose in others. The toll of death and destruction was indescribable.

"When some semblance of stability returned, the survivors looked out upon a new Earth. The continent of Mu was no more. Only scattered islands remained in a vast and empty ocean. Around the world, people reverted to primitive survival and began the arduous climb toward civilization again. In many places the Mu were blamed for what had happened and they had to go into hiding to escape persecution. These lonely, scattered groups gave rise to later stories of magical 'little people' found in almost every culture. The orders they created continued without them, except for rare contact by a very limited number of adepts.

"Other civilizations rose and fell. Among them was brilliant Atlantis, which almost achieved world domination before, in lesser imitation of Mu, it tore itself apart in a war that sent it to the bottom of the ocean. Meanwhile, the tradition of Huna was carried on by small groups who clothed the teaching in the culture of their locations. The majority of these lost contact with one another, but they continued to teach and heal and train. In some cases they were able to keep the simplicity of Huna intact, and in others distortions entered to the point that the fundamental knowledge was virtually lost, and good practices were carried on with a false understanding of their nature.

"After the disruption caused by the fall of Mu,

survivors in the Pacific Basin, whom we now call Polynesians, gathered at two places to rebuild their societies—Samoa and the Society Islands. Among them were members of the three orders who acted as priests, healers and technical experts. Only the Intuitionists maintained contact with their colleagues in the rest of the world. Slowly, they built their technology up to the point where they could build great sailing vessels capable of carrying a hundred people or more, and they set off to explore what remained of Mu. For the most part, they stayed within the rough boundaries of the old continent, making only occasional forays into bordering lands.

"The group that successfully ventured the furthest outside of those boundaries was the Maori, who settled in New Zealand. The name Maori means 'the true people' or the original inhabitants, and refers both to their origin from the old continent of Mu (as mixed descendants of the star race) and to the fact that they were the first people to settle the new lands they discovered. They soon lost touch with the other Polynesians, and except for memories in old chants and songs the two groups forgot about each other until Western explorers brought them together again.

"Another group, following ancient navigational information contained in traditional chants, struck north from Tahiti and the Marquesas to land and settle in the Hawaiian Islands. The first island they landed at was Kauai, oldest of the main islands, and there they discovered some of the original Menehune people, whom they also called the Mu. These Mu were very shy, but not unfriendly, and were sometimes helpful to the newcomers. They had stone temples and waterways and were experts at irrigation and building fishponds.

14

For many years the two peoples got along fairly well together and there was considerable intermarriage. It was this last point, however, that led the king of the Mu to make a harsh decision. He saw that if the intermarriage continued the Mu would disappear as a separate people, so he decided that they would have to leave. Tradition says that one night all the Mu departed from the north end of Kauai, but no one knows how or where they went.

"At first the three orders of kahunas in Hawaii were on an equal basis and commerce continued between Hawaii, Samoa and Tahiti. In the thirteenth century A.D., though, a power-hungry kahuna of the order of Emotionals came from Samoa, ostensibly to help a reorganization of the Emotionals of Hawaii. In a short time he succeeded in gaining religious and political control of the islands, with the result that contact between Hawaii and the rest of Polynesia came to a halt; the building of the great sea-going vessels was stopped; the navigational and astronomical schools were abandoned; the people became subject to a religion of superstition and restriction. The Intellectual order suffered the most and much knowledge was lost. The Intuitionists were forced into hiding for the most part, and many Emotionals turned increasingly to distorted practices. For six hundred years the people of Hawaii were subject to harsh rule, psychic terrorism and much social turmoil. By the time Captain Cook arrived, all the islands were engaged in war. The idyllic nature of Polynesian life was largely a myth perpetuated by foreigners who couldn't see below the surface.

"Throughout all of this, a small group of Intuitionists maintained telepathic contact with the rest of their order around the world, and were content to work behind the scenes for the good of mankind. Now the times have changed, and because of the rapidity of communication, the expansion of consciousness in much of the world, and the growing understanding of alternate realities, it is felt that the knowledge of Huna needs to be spread as far and wide as possible."

 CHAPTER 1

The Kahunas

Since the time of early European explorations in the Pacific Ocean, the Western world has built up a romantic image of the South Seas based on the concept of a simple, carefree, primitive society. It has been the dream of many men to chuck the burdens of job and family and run away to a tropical island where all you have to do is lie in a hammock sipping fruit punch while the childlike natives take care of your every need. Another Western attitude, less romantic, is that before the blessings of civilization were brought to them, the people of the islands were ignorant savages governed by superstitious fear and undisciplined sensuality. Along with this attitude is the idea that these people had no philosophical thought to speak of, no developed abstract concepts, no art that was more than decorative, no books of any kind, and certainly no science or technology worth mentioning.

The truth of the matter, established by scientific research in many fields, is that the societies of Polynesia were every bit as complex as is our own: their moral, ethical and legal codes as stringent; their philosophies as developed; their art and literature as rich; and their science as skilled. However, the direction in which they developed these aspects was unique. As modern social psychologists point out, if we try to judge the accomplishments of other cultures by using our own as a standard, we risk distorting that judgment and severely limiting any benefit we might derive from contact with the culture we are judging. And the culture of Polynesia has aspects that can benefit us in every area of life.

The People of Polynesia

Polynesia is a term applied equally to a geographical area and to a people who share a common historical, linguistic, cultural and physical background. The area is usually defined as a triangle stretching from New Zealand in the southwest Pacific, to Hawaii in the north, down to Easter Island in the southeast, and back to New Zealand. It is an immense area, larger than the continent of South America, and dotted with volcanic and coral islands that are often as much as two thousand miles apart. What is remarkable is that this whole area was explored, settled and had regular commerce between the islands for hundreds and possibly thousands of years before Columbus made his voyage across the Atlantic.

The people of this area, the Polynesians, comprise the Maori, Samoans, Tongans, Tahitians, Marquesans, Hawaiians, Easter Islanders and others, named for the most part in modern times after their location. Though these groups are separated by vast distances, and in some cases have been out of contact with one another for centuries, there are fewer cultural differences between them than between such close neighbors as the French and the Germans. A thin-nosed Maori and a broad-nosed Hawaiian may not look like brothers, and their environmentally shaped ways of life may vary considerably, but they share the same basic language, cultural heroes, legends and inner knowledge. And they accept each other as coming from the same original stock, as Peter Buck, a part Maori traveler, found when he voyaged to other islands that hadn't been contacted by an "outside" Polynesian in living memory.

A question that remains unsettled among anthropologists is the original homeland of the Polynesians, along with the question of what route they took to get to their present home. The most favored modern theory is that they came from Indonesia, or possibly India, and passed through the west Pacific island groups of Micronesia or Melanesia on their way. This is based partly on some minor linguistic similarities, the supposed origin of many plants used by the Polynesians, a few technological similarities, and the notion that, since they had to come from somewhere, Asia was the most likely place.

Max Freedom Long and others have proposed that the original homeland of the Polynesians was in the Near East. Long based his idea on an unverified story from an Englishman who lived with a Berber tribe in the Sahara. This tribe claimed to have been part of a group that had built the pyramids of Egypt; they had split off from the rest of the group who went to the Pacific to seek a new land. However, I spent some four and a half years, off and on, with the Berbers, and was unable to verify such a tradition. More importantly, Long impressively used linguistic studies to show that kahuna knowledge was incorporated into parts of the Old and New Testaments of the Bible. He even went so far as to trace a route for the Pacific-destined group down the

Red Sea, along the coast of Africa to Madagascar (whose language, Malagasy, does have affinities with Polynesian), across the ocean to India, and thence through Indonesia to the Pacific, using philosophical similarities as his main argument. Yet another Polynesian homeland has been proposed by Thor Heyerdahl of *Kon Tiki* fame, who sought to prove in a practical way that the Polynesians could have come from South America.

As noted in the prologue, my kahuna mentor, WK, has a considerably different version, supported to a great extent by researchers like James Churchward, author of a number of books about the continent of Mu, and Leinani Melville, author of *Children of the Rainbow*. It claims that Polynesia was the *source* of cultural similarities elsewhere and not the end recipient. Of course, there can be as much doubt about this version as any other, but it does have the virtue of being a Polynesian version and it does answer many questions. It explains for instance, why the extremely skilled Polynesian navigators never settled any area outside the afore-mentioned triangle, how kahuna knowledge could have traveled throughout the world without being accompanied by the Polynesians, and how such subgroups as the Maori in New Zealand could have ancient navigation chants that gave sailing directions to Hawaii. It also explains why groups like the Maori, Hawaiians and Easter Islanders tell in their legends of people who were living in the islands when they first landed there. In Hawaiian, these people are even called the Mu, and there are many tales of conflict and cooperation with them. On the island of Kauai in the Hawaiian chain, I have seen temple floors and stoneworks that resemble pre-Incan building styles much more than they do anything built by early Polynesian settlers. These were supposedly built by the Mu people, also known as the Menehune.

The Kapu System

The question of origin may never be answered to everyone's satisfaction, but it is a fact that the Polynesians were there when the Europeans arrived in Polynesia. Among other things, the first Western explorers found a powerful group of people known as *kahunas* who were the religious leaders, master artists and craftsmen, doctors, lawyers, teachers and political advisors of the society. They and the chiefly families ruled the people by what has come to be called the *kapu* system, though most Westerners would be more familiar with the Tongan form of the word, *tabu* or *taboo*.

The *kapu* system has been much maligned because it has been so little understood. The word *kapu* has usually been taken to mean "forbidden" and has been associated with mysterious warnings regarding things outside the scope of reason. A fuller rendering of the word, however, would also include the meanings of "sacred, holy, or consecrated." The *kapu* system was actually a code of laws, like that which is necessary for any society to function smoothly. A certain grove of trees or a special fishing place might be declared *kapu* for one or more seasons to keep it from being overexploited, for instance. This is no different from our present regulated hunting and fishing seasons, but such environmental foresight was totally unknown to the early European visitors to Polynesia who couldn't undersand why one tree or place was *kapu* and another was not. Certain parts of a temple or plots of land could also be declared *kapu* because they were reserved for priestly or chiefly use. The path to such a place would be marked by a pair of crossed sticks topped by a ball of white cloth, and the natives would refuse to pass beyond such a marker because the breaking of *kapu* laws was severely punished. Yet, the same European who would hesitate greatly before violating a royal or government sign marked "Keep Out" or "No Trespassing" in his own country would often think the island native was merely acting out of superstition.

The most difficult *kapus* to understand for the foreigner were, of course, those that dealt with social customs. In some parts of Polynesia there was a *kapu* punishable by death against allowing the shadow of a commoner to fall upon that of a chief. This seems the rankest kind of superstition at first, but the foreigner would not be likely to know that the word for *shadow* also has the meaning of "laughter," and that the above event could be interpreted as an act of sedition or *lese majeste*. Another *kapu* forbade women to eat bananas, because the word for banana is similar to the word for genitals and the act would have been as offensive as using four-letter sexual words in public has traditionally been in the United States.

The *kapu*, then, formed the basis for the Polynesian legal system. At its best it reinforced the cohesiveness and productivity of the society, but the system could be, and often was, used by greedy chiefs and priests for political and economic exploitation. Social rebellions and/or emigrations were not uncommonly inspired by overly restrictive *kapus* imposed on the people by their leaders. The severity of the *kapus* enacted by Kamehameha the Great to maintain control over his Hawaiian kingdom, the unreasonable exploitation of those *kapus* by certain kahuna priests, and the psychic misinterpretation of an opportunistic kahuna leader were some of the main reasons why the whole *kapu* system in Hawaii was so easily overthrown in the time of Kamehameha's son.

The Kahunas Of Hawaii

Since I have had more experience with Hawaiian kahunas than with Tahitian *tahunas* or Maori *tohungas*, the following section will deal with the Hawaiian system, based on historical record and discussions with WK.

When Captain James Cook anchored off the leeward coast of Kauai on January 19, 1778, he broke a six-hundred-year isolation of the Hawaiian islands from the rest of the world. Contrary to popular belief, however, Cook and those who followed did not intrude on a simple island paradise. The beauty of these volcanic islands was breathtaking, and when the inhabitants were friendly they were very friendly. But the Hawaiians were neither uncorrupted innocents nor ignorant savages. Their society was structured as a full-blown feudal system, and Cook arrived in the midst of violent social and political turmoil. After the first brief shock of contact, the Europeans and their superior technology were quickly exploited for political purposes by the pragmatic Hawaiian leaders, including the kahunas.

In history books much has been made of the story that Captain Cook was thought to be the god *Lono* returning to the islands. According to the Hawaiian historian Kamakau, the people of Kauai were astounded and frightened at the unprecedented sight of British ships standing off the shore. The people had no idea who was in the ships. It was a kahuna, Kuohu, who decided that the ships had to be the temple and altars of *Lono* because the masts and sails resembled the pole and banners used in an annual ceremony dedicated to that god. Cook and his men stepped ashore for a short visit and then took off for the coast of America. Word spread quickly through the islands, and by the time Cook returned to stop at Kealakekua Bay on the Big Island of Hawaii, the stage was set for a remarkably astute political maneuver, which might have been successful if Cook had not stayed so long.

Cook's second arrival happened to take place in an area sacred to *Lono* and toward the end of the annual festival dedicated to him. There are no records of what I am about to suggest and WK says he knows of no tradition for or against it, but the coincidence of when and where Cook landed the second time is so great that I suspect the kahunas had a hand in it. As we shall see later, they undoubtedly had the capability of clair-voyantly knowing where Cook was and of sending telepathic messages to guide him right to the bay where thousands of people had gathered for the *Lono* festival. Cook remarked in his journal that he had never seen such a large gathering of people in all the islands. Since the king of the island of Hawaii was in the process of con-solidating his power over the people as part of his war effort against Maui, it was probably at the suggestion of his kahuna advisors that Cook was acclaimed as the god *Lono* himself come to lend his *mana* (divine power) to the side that was obviously in the right. The chiefs and the kahunas were not fools. They could recognize superior technology, however strange; they knew a man when they saw one; and they also knew how to take advantage of an opportunity. Unfortunately, the longer Cook stayed, the harder it was to keep up the pretense that he was a god. When he finally left after a few weeks, they showed undisguised relief. Unfortunately, Cook had to return again after only a week to repair a broken foremast. By this time the festival was over, the people had been dispersed, and Cook's reception was decidedly frosty. Relations between the Hawaiians and the Europeans rapidly deteriorated over the next two weeks until Cook tried to take the highly sacred person of the king as hostage for a relatively minor theft by one of the king's subjects. A battle ensued on the beach and Cook was killed. The point is that Cook's designation as the god *Lono* was no more than a politically inspired farce intended to gain favor for the regime of King Kalaniopuu. The chiefs and kahunas knew better, but at this stage in Hawaiian history the "state religion" was only a political tool designed to increase the power of the chiefs and certain priests, and to exploit the masses.

As more and more Europeans began to visit the islands, they heard tales of strange powers exerted by certain people known as kahunas. Stories of telepathy, clairvoyance, healing by touch, the causing of death at a distance, and walking over burning lava were mixed with observations of exotic ceremonies and chants, the practice of massage and herbal medicine, and the apparent worship of grotesque idols. It was easy to label these stories as pure superstition until one became directly involved in a personal experience. Then, for the thinking person, it was clear that something strange indeed was going on behind the religious facade. There was no doubt that some kahunas, at least, were able to do things that seemed outside the scope of physical laws. The longer one lived in the islands, the more one grew to accept this as fact.

However, because of four main factors, it wasn't easy to find out what was really going on. First was the natural reluctance of the scientifically trained Westerner to accept such abilities as possible. To do so would be to plunge back into the Dark Ages of magic and superstition that the Western world was still struggling out of. Second was the natural tendency of Christian-oriented visitors to blame all such things on the work of the Devil, for how else could ignorant heathens have such powers?

Third was the fact that, by the time of the arrival of the first Europeans, the mainstream kahuna practices were quite corrupt, and most of the early knowledge had been lost. While a small group retained the ancient teachings virtually intact, the majority of the kahunas—especially those involved in politics—had degenerated into a mere ceremonial priesthood, with very few members who even knew the rudiments of such things as telepathy and clairvoyance. This is poignantly brought out in the story of Hewahewa, high priest of Kamehameha II. In 1819, shortly after the death of Kamehameha I, this prominent kahuna in charge of the king's war god image had a vision in which he saw the representatives of what seemed to be a much more powerful god landing on the shores of Hawaii. No doubt influenced by his acquaintance with superior European technology and tales of Christianity, Hewahewa set about gaining support from fellow kahunas, ambitious chiefs and dissatisfied royal wives for nothing less than the abolition of the *kapu* system and the overthrow of the old gods. In this way he hoped to ingratiate himself with the representatives of the new god and at the same time undercut the power of any kahuna rivals. Kamehameha II, unlike his father, was a weak-willed man, and by November of 1819 he gave in to the urgings of Hewahewa and his followers. By the apparently simple act of sitting down to eat with the women, Kamehameha II broke a serious *kapu* and set a precedent for chiefs and commoners alike. The word was spread throughout the now united island chain and the people, long oppressed by overly severe *kapus*, gave vent to their feelings by burning and tearing down temples and statues. One kahuna rival of Hewahewa tried to prevent it, but he and his supporters were roundly beaten in a battle. For six months, then, Hawaii was a land without a religion and without laws. It was a time of great confusion, because without the *kapus* and without the gods there were no firm guidelines for conduct and no psychological security.

Finally, in 1820, the first Christian missionaries from Boston landed where Hewahewa said they would. He and his fellow kahunas were on hand with many sick and lame persons they had brought for the new god to heal. They sang a chant of welcome and asked the missionaries to show the power of their new god by healing the sick. Of course, the missionaries could do no such thing, and after a great deal of confusion on both sides Hewahewa was forced to realize that he had wrongly interpreted his vision and had destroyed the whole formal religious and legal structure of his nation for nothing. He is known to the history books as Hewahewa, but that cannot have been his real name. The Hawaiians have always been very careful about choosing personal names based on their meaning. It seems obvious that the unfortunate high priest was given the name of Hewahewa after he made his terrible error, because it means "the crazy one who failed to recognize something."

The fourth factor that interfered with an early understanding of kahuna knowledge was the outlawing of all kahuna practices by the Christian missionaries-turned-politicians as soon as they had the power to do so. According to Max Long, who lived in the islands while this law was in effect, the law of Hawaii concerning the use of magic to heal read as follows:

> "Section 1034. Sorcery—Penalty. Any person who shall attempt the cure of another by practice of sorcery, witchcraft, *anaana, hoopiopio, hoounauna,* or *hoomanamana* (terms describing psychic practices), or other superstitious or deceitful methods, shall, upon conviction thereof, be fined in a sum not less than one hundred dollars or be imprisoned not to exceed six months at hard labor." There is also another section of the law which classes the kahuna with bunco men and defines him as one posing as a kahuna, taking money under pretense of having magical power, or *admitting* that he is a kahuna. For this the fine goes up to a thousand dollars and a year in prison.[1]

Needless to say, this was enough to drive all true kahunas into hiding and to make it extremely difficult for a non-Hawaiian to gain any access to kahuna knowledge. In spite of the law, though, both Hawaiian and unprejudiced non-Hawaiians continued to seek out and receive help from kahunas whose identity was well-protected, and pseudo-kahunas were frequently trotted out for civic ceremonies and tourists. Only recently has the law been modified so that, while it still provides safeguards against fraud, it is no longer a crime to be or claim to be a kahuna.

The self-destruction of their own religious traditions and the powerful impact of Christianity and Western technology caused most Hawaiians to reject kahuna influence and teachings. Kahuna knowledge was traditionally passed on to a carefully selected natural or adopted child, but the above factors, along with non-Hawaiian intermarriages and the decimation of the population through introduced diseases, left a very small number willing or able to carry on in their parents' footsteps.

And yet, amidst all the difficulties, there remained a core of active kahunas who continued to carry on the practices of mental, emotional and physical healing; helping individuals to change the future; and even the greatly feared "death prayer." No less a personage than the curator of the Bishop Museum in Honolulu, William Tufts Brigham, engaged himself for years in trying to uncover the secret of what he knew were valid kahuna practices. He had personal experiences with fire-walking, healing and the telepathic death prayer, and was convinced beyond a doubt that some knowledge highly important to humanity was still waiting to be tapped. He was never successful in his quest, but before his death he left to Max Long a legacy of what he had learned, which can be summed up as follows:

> I have been able to prove that none of the popular explanations of kahuna magic will hold water. It is not suggestion, nor anything yet known in psychology. They use something that we have still to discover, and this is something inestimably important. We simply must find it. It will revolutionize the world if we can find it. It will change the entire concept of science. It would bring order to conflicting religious beliefs. . . .
>
> Always keep watch for three things in the study of this magic. There must be some form of consciousness back of, and directing, the processes of magic. Controlling the heat in fire-walking, for example. There must also be some form of force used in exerting this control, if we can but recognize it. And last, there must be some form of substance, visible or invisible, through which the force can act. Watch always for these, and if you can find any one, it may lead to the others.[2]

Long continued the search along these lines and, although he never studied under a kahuna, over a period of many years he discovered the three elements outlined by Brigham, conducted experiments to prove their existence, found correlations with the discoveries of others elsewhere, and discovered further that the kahuna system of knowledge was not limited to Polynesia, but was spread over the world. It was a remarkable feat and it made the main elements of this knowledge available to the public for the first time.

The kinds of things that kahunas deal with regularly have now become the subject of increasingly widespread scientific investigation and popular interest. There are laboratories studying mind-to-mind communication, the phenomena of altered states of consciousness, and psychokinetic influence on matter, while more and more brave doctors and psychotherapists are experimenting with unusual healing methods such as guided imagery, pressure therapy and the transfer of energy from one person to another. Aside from conservative resistance to all this, the investigations are hindered by the lack of a coherent or unified theory to explain how such practices work. The kahuna system provides both working practices and a good working theory.

The Kahuna Orders

Kahuna is a word that has suffered distortion in modern times. Originally intended to refer to a trained adept, an expert caretaker and transmitter of knowledge and power, it has been applied more recently to priests and ministers of Western religions, psychics, healers and even the leaders of surfing clubs. While such use may be understandable because these people may be experts at what they know, WK insists that a true kahuna is one who has been initiated by a natural or adoptive parent and trained in an organized body of esoteric knowledge as part of an identifiable group. The use of the word to mean "priest, minister or leader" is a modern extension of the meaning based on misunderstanding. The same is true of its application to natural psychics and healers who may or may not have received knowledge from their parents. The Hawaiians had many names for those who use psychic abilities. Some of these are:

kaula—prophet or magician	*po'ko'i*—sorcerer
ho'ola—healer	*mo'okiko*—evil sorcerer
ho'okalakupua—magician or adept	*kilo 'uhane*—spiritualist
	ho'ike papulua—psychic

The above terms were applied to those who exercised such powers without being a kahuna. The latter might do the same things, but as a trained expert belonging to a traditional order. In such a case one would be called a *kahuna kaula, kahuna ho'ola,* etc. Furthermore, various types of kahunas were trained to be experts in things that we would not consider esoteric at all today, such as navigation, medicine, engineering and meteorology. The kahunas were the scientists and technical experts of their day, but their knowledge extended into realms which are just beginning to be tapped in the Western world on a large scale. For instance, a navigator would not only be technically skilled, but he would be trained to communicate with the wind and the waves as well.

Originally, there was no structured hierarchy among the kahunas, and this is still the case with two of the orders to be described below. Actually, the orders were and are more like medieval guilds than religious orders in the Western Christian tradition. A kahuna achieves prominence, not by promotion, inheritance or even election, but through respect for his abilities and knowledge. The highest "position" a kahuna can aspire to is *puhi okaoka*, which refers to one well versed in all branches of knowledge. Since kahunas have no structured authority over each other, they are sought out and followed because of what they can do and what they know.

At some point in history the kahunas became divided into three broadly defined orders, as noted by WK in the prologue. Each of these emphasized a particular approach to knowledge and practice, but the difference had less to do with function than with technique. All three made use of the elements of magic discovered by Max Long, and their areas of expertise overlapped considerably. With this in mind, let's look at each of the orders in turn.

The Order of Ku.

This order was called "the Emotionals" by WK and it emphasizes a sensual/emotional approach to life. In terms of healing, the kahunas of this order are more prone to use exercise, massage and the laying-on-of-hands as methods of treatment. Like psychotherapy, these techniques tend toward the release of repressed emotions and the uncovering of past events that led to present problems. Concerning the environment, the approach is mainly one of attempting direct control over events and circumstances through the use of willpower and influencing other people's emotions. Sports, politics, commerce and war, as well as organized and and ceremonial religion, have been the natural interests for kahunas of this order. This is the order that came to dominate Hawaii after the arrival of the powerful kahuna Paao from Samoa in about 1275 A.D. He instituted a strict hierarchy in the order of Ku and introduced human sacrifice, a practice which is decidedly not a part of kahuna tradition. After the arrival of Paao and the chief he installed, all traffic between Hawaii and the outside world ceased until the arrival of Captain Cook.

The Order of Lono.

The approach of this order, WK's "Intellectuals," is intellectual/mechanical. In Hawaii it produced the herbal doctors and surgeons, the agriculturalists, the navigators, the astronomers and astrologers, the meteorologists, and the shipwrights who guided the construction of the great ocean-going canoes. In healing and psychotherapy, these kahunas emphasize the use of herbs and drugs, diet, and natural sources of healing energy such as sunlight, sea salt, crystals and special locations discovered through the use of geomancy (a form of divination using supposed energy currents in the earth). They see the environment as something to be manipulated by understanding the mechanics of its operation. In Hawaii, this order suffered the most under the domination of the order of Ku, and by the time the Europeans arrived many of their arts were lost.

The Order of Kane.

These "Intuitionists" have an approach which is spiritual/integrative. The techniques used by the other two orders are considered as temporary tools to be applied until one reaches the basic understanding that the outer world is merely a reflection of thought. The emphasis is on a unification or integration of spirit, mind and body for the purpose of self-mastery, with the implication that self-mastery is the key to a mastery of life. In healing, primary importance is given to the effects of thoughts upon the body, and presently held beliefs are looked upon as more influential than past experiences. The environment is seen as an extension of the body, equally influenced by thoughts and beliefs. Imagination is the most important tool of this order, and much of the training concerns its disciplined use. These kahunas work with alternate states of consciousness and the refined use of psychic abilities more than do those of the other orders. They could be considered as pragmatic philosophers, and in numbers they have always been smaller than the kahunas of Ku and Lono. They suffered little in Hawaii under the Ku domination because, in a manner of speaking, they merely went "underground." According to WK they maintained contact with the rest of the world through telepathy. This is the order into which my father was initiated and in which I received my training.

The Renegades

The most feared phenomenon in old Hawaii was the "death prayer," a form of destructive emotional telepathy often combined with negative suggestion. Virtually all the kahunas who engaged in this were renegades from the order of Ku, though there were non-kahuna sorcerers who practiced it, too. The most common epithet applied to them was *kahuna 'ai pilau* (kahunas who are eaters of filth). Either to gain power over others or simply for pay, they used their knowledge of psychism, psychology and emotional energy to injure or kill. As William Brigham knew, much more than simple suggestion was used. The death prayer could work whether or not there was conscious knowledge of what was going on, but this practice did require considerable skill on the part of the practitioner, and suggestion was used whenever possible to make it easier. Fortunately, each order had a number of kahunas who were specialists in *oki* or *kala*, forms of counter-magic which cut off the death prayer and rendered it harmless.

The Kahunas Today

WK estimates that there are probably not more than twenty-five genuine kahunas in Hawaii today, only a half-dozen of whom are of the order of Kane. The rest are about evenly divided between Ku and Lono. However, many of those who call themselves kahunas are merely individual psychics and healers or those who give the tourists a show. With a few exceptions, the genuine kahunas have either retreated completely from society or have integrated themselves into it, so that no one realizes who they are or what they can do. The knowledge is alive and operating but not obvious. And contrary to what many tourists seem to think, Hawaiian ancestry does not confer kahuna knowledge. Even Leinani Melville has written that practically no Hawaiian or part-Hawaiian has any understanding of what Huna, the kahuna knowledge, is all about. Outside of Hawaii, kahunas are also rare or very much concealed. I met a Maori kahuna who said that the inner knowledge is almost gone from his people, and my kahuna teacher in Africa had only three apprentices during the nearly seven years that I knew him. My attempts to contact kahunas that my father knew in England were unsuccessful.

It has upset some Hawaiians that I call myself a kahuna because I don't have a drop of Hawaiian blood in my body, even though there is plenty of precedent in Hawaiian legend and history for non-Polynesians to have been made kahunas. Of course, anyone can claim to be a kahuna, but a long time ago someone that WK and I consider a great kahuna told us to use this test: "Ye shall know them by their fruits."

 CHAPTER 2

The Inner Tradition

Kahuna philosophy can be summed up in four state-ments, each represented by a single Hawaiian keyword:

1. "You create your own reality (*Ike*)." This means your personal experience of reality, every part of it. You create it through your beliefs, expectations, attitudes, desires, fears, judgments, interpretations, feelings, intentions and consistent or persistent thoughts.

2. "You get what you concentrate on (*Makia*)." The thoughts and feelings that you dwell on, in full aware-ness or not, form the blueprint for bringing into your life the nearest available equivalent experience to those same thoughts and feelings.

3. "You are unlimited (*Kala*)." There are no bound-aries to your selfhood, no boundaries between you and your body, you and the world, or you and God. Any divisions used for discussion are terms of function and/or convenience because separateness

is only a useful illusion.

4. "Your moment of power is now (*Manawa*)." You are not bound by any experience of the past or any perception of the future, for the past is only a memory and the future a mere possibility. You have the power in the present moment to change limiting beliefs and consciously plant the seeds for a future of your choosing. As you change your mind, you change your experience.

These ideas are not unique to the kahunas. In fact, I borrowed the phrases used to translate the Huna concepts from *Seth*/Jane Roberts because they fit so well, but the ideas conveyed by the words can be found in many places in the writings of many times. However, they have never been very popular because they declare that without exception the individual is responsible for his personal experience, and this can be viewed as subversive by rulers and intolerable by subjects. Curiously, the uneasiness produced by the implication of responsibility often blinds people to the implication of tremendous freedom which the philosophy also contains.

In the sections below I will cover other aspects of kahuna philosophy that are linked to the ones given above. For this material, as well as that of all the chapters to follow, I will draw upon my own training as a kahuna of the Order of Kane, on personal field and literary research, and from discussions with WK.

The Kahuna "Bible"

Much of kahuna philosophy is embodied in the so-called "Creation Chant," also called the *Kumulipo*, which is as close to a kahuna "bible" as anything available today. Originally part of an oral tradition that was passed on by kahunas trained in perfect memory, it was probably compiled in more or less its present form in 1700 by the kahuna Keaulumoku. All the translations that have been made (which are not very many) are from a written manuscript that was once the property of King Kalakaua, who was very interested in preserving Hawaiian traditions, including the secrets of Huna and the role of kahunas as healers.

In kahuna philosophy, both spiritual and material worlds take shape as a result of an interplay between relative forces, often represented by a male and a female. For every "god" in the Hawaiian pantheon, with few exceptions, there is a female counterpart to help with creation. Many of these are named in the first seven sections of the *Kumulipo*, along with verses that seem to tell of the formation of plant and animal life on earth. The eighth and ninth chants or sections apparently tell of the birth of man into conscious awareness and of his multiplying over the earth. The rest of the total of sixteen sections in the Kalakaua version seem to be mainly genealogies, except for an account of the cultural hero, Maui.

A problem that scholars have with the *Kumulipo*, however, is that they cannot agree on how it should be translated. In an oral tradition with a language like Hawaiian, much depends on subtleties of pronunciation and context that cannot adequately be transmitted by written words. To make it even harder, the kahunas had the habit of incorporating several layers of meaning into their chants, which was done by the chiefs even in their love songs. During a visit with kahuna friends in Hawaii, I was told that the *Kumulipo* has seven layers of meaning, and I was given a key to one layer which I am presently working on. When I asked why they didn't translate it themselves, they said they did not have as much experience as I with translations, didn't enjoy it as much, and that they had better things to do.

To give an example of what is involved, here is the first line from the *Kumulipo*:

O ke au i kahuli wela ka honua

and here are several ways it has already been translated:

The wheel of time turns to the burnt-out remains of the world.

Adolf Bastion

At the time that turned the heat of the earth.
Queen Liliuokalani

The time when the earth was hotly changed.
Kakahi

At the time when the earth became hot.
Martha Beckwith

At the time when this earth evolved as a flaming ball of fire.
Leinani Melville

Without denying that any of the above may be correct, here are three more that I have made. The last one is part of the translation on which I am currently working:

There was a time when the land was violently changed.

The active seed transformed the earth with passion.

Thought changes earthly things.

The God Concept

The popular religion of Hawaii was filled with gods and goddesses, ghosts, fairies, elves, sprites and spirits who could change shape at will and who might be friendly or unfriendly toward man, depending on how they were treated. However, this popular view was only a distortion of kahuna knowledge.

When the early missionaries to Hawaii were trying to understand the language of the islanders, they came across concepts so foreign to their thinking that certain words were given quite unjustified definitions. One of these was *akua*, which was translated as *god*. When the missionaries asked the Hawaiians their name for the big statues which appeared to be objects of worship, the natives told them the name was *akua*. When they were asked who or what they prayed to for advice, protection, or accomplishment, they said *akua*. But the missionaries got confused when the Hawaiians applied the same word to things that didn't seem godlike at all, including the despised caste of slaves. As the missionary Lorrin Andrews wrote in his dictionary of Hawaiian in 1865, "the term, on the visit of foreigners, was applied to artificial objects, the nature or property of which Hawaiians did not understand, as the movement of a watch, a compass, the self-striking of a clock, etc." Based on the fact that *akua* was also the name for the night of the full moon, Andrews also said, "It would seem that the ancient idea of an *akua* embraced something incomprehensible, powerful, and yet complete."[3] In this Andrews was on the right track, but he and most Westerners since have dismissed the apparent anomalies and have continued to think that the Hawaiians and their kahunas simply worshipped idols that they called gods.

The truth, vitally important for understanding the philosophy and practices of the kahunas, is that *akua* means "a fully formed idea-in-action." It is an active idea that manifests effects. The roots of the word contain meanings that have to do with motion or tendency from oneself outward, transformation, and completed action. The kahunas knowingly utilized certain of these idea structures for their healing. The four greatest *akua* were *Kane, Ku, Lono* and *Kanaloa*. If you can conceive that a particular kind of idea can be an intelligent energy essence, then these might legitimately be called gods, but not otherwise.

Kane

Outwardly, *Kane* was considered as the highest, most spiritual god and was never represented by a carved image. At the most, he would be represented by a natural object, usually an undressed upright stone. He was thought of as a god of peace and love, and his female counterpart was *Wahine*. In ordinary conversation, *kane* means "man" and *wahine* means "woman." *Kane* and *Wahine* were therefore symbols for the equivalent Chinese concept of yin and yang. For the kahunas, *Kane* and his mate represented the dual-natured god-self of each human being, similar to the "Christ within" of the Christians or the Buddha Mind of the Buddhists. He/she is, in other words, the spiritual essence and source of the individual, the soul, Higher Self or Greater Self. Another term for this "personal god" is *aumakua*, which Long nicely translated as "utterly trustworthy parental spirit"; and two other terms for the same concept, *kumupa'a* and *'ao'ao*, both carry connotations of a teacher and guide. By the time of the arrival of the Europeans in Hawaii, most Hawaiians revered this inner spirit only as a kind of guardian ancestor because people had mixed up their physical source of their existence with their spiritual one. I will have more to say about this *akua* and the next two *akuas* in the chapter on the kahunas' mind/body approach to healing.

Ku

Ku was outwardly associated with fertility, rain, sorcery and war. As a common word, its meanings have to do with generative symbology; a base or framework for something; a thing which can be changed or transformed; and something which can have emotional complexes. Psychologically, *Ku* stands for what may be called the "body-mind"; the organizing consciousness of the body, the receiver of information about the physical world (seen and unseen), and the executor of action. It is tempting to call it the "subconscious," as I have done elsewhere, but unless the integral association with the body is understood, that term can be misleading. In nearly any tourist shop in Hawaii you can buy a cast figure of *Ku* that is a beautiful example of kahuna symbol "writing." The statuette for this *akua* shows a being with virtually no headdress (its province is memory imagination), streamers reaching down to the ground (primary involvement with the physical world), and closed eyes (limited awareness).

Lono

Lono was the god of agriculture, medicine and meteorology in the outer religion. In kahuna psychology he represents the intellect, that portion of the mind which perceives, interprets and directs. A code or root breakdown of the name reveals meanings of receiving information and acting on it; brains, especially the forebrain, and intelligence; reaching for goals; creating desires; and imaginative thought. The statuette of *Lono* is a being with a high headdress (creative imagination), short streamers not reaching the ground (indirect contact with the physical), and no eyes (dependent on something else for information about the world).

Kanaloa

In the most ancient Hawaiian legends, *Kanaloa* is always mentioned as the companion of *Kane*, and both traveled around the islands finding springs of water. *Kanaloa* was known as a god of healing and a god of the oceans, and he was often represented by an octopus or squid as well as a particular carved figure. The use of the octopus/squid as a symbol has to do with the sacred significance of the number eight and the fact that the word for both creatures, *he'e*, means "to flow (as in the flowing of the life force)" and "to flee (as in the fleeing away of sickness)." After Christian influence entered the islands, *Kane, Ku* and *Lono* were equated with the Trinity, and *Kanaloa* was made to assume the role of Satan.

As a word, *kanaloa* means "secure, firm, unconquerable," and is used as a poetic reference for food, a symbol for power. In the inner kahuna tradition *Kanaloa* represents the Ideal Man—fully aware, fully physical, and at the same time fully spiritual, loving and being loved and in conscious contact with his source. The carved figure shows a being with a high headdress (the power of creative thought), streamers reaching down to the ground (direct involvement with the physical), and eyes wide open (complete awareness of the spiritual and physical worlds).

Triune Man

In kahuna philosophy and psychology, man is a spiritual being with three aspects represented by *Kane*,

Ku and *Lono*. In the ideal state the three function as one, represented by *Kanaloa*, and in this state man is able to express his full potential. For reasons to be gone into in later chapters, disunity can occur, causing a breakdown in communication among the three aspects and a lessening of man's effectiveness in life. To regain this effectiveness, the kahunas first teach how to reunite *Lono* and *Ku*, the intellect and the body, or the conscious and subconscious minds. To the degree that this re-unification is successful, union with *Kane* also occurs. Of course, it is not a physical reunification that is meant because there is no real separation, but a reunification through increased awareness. Symbolically, when the carved figures of *Lono* and *Ku* are combined, the result is *Kanaloa*, the companion of God.

The Godhead

When *Kane* is referred to as God, it is the very personal god-self of the individual that is meant. The kahunas also recognize an ultimate, infinite God or Godhead, and one of the terms for this is *Kumulipo*, the same word used for the Creation Chant and which can be translated as "source of life." *Kumulipo* is considered as immanent in nature, and the inherent oneness of all things is accepted as a basic truth. As beings focused in physical reality, however, the kahunas feel that this world is the most practical object for study and development. Their view of this world is much broader than is traditional in Western culture, and their perception of it involves viewpoints from several states of consciousness, so they feel there is plenty of room for work in the here-and-now without useless speculation on the nature of the Godhead. Huna is a pragmatic philosophy, and there are no theologians among the kahunas. *Kumulipo* is all that is, infinite, inherently loving. Not much more that is useful can be said about it.

Spirits

The personal god or god-self (*Kane* or *aumakua*) is not limited to mankind in kahuna philosophy. Since God is in everything (or everything is in God—kahunas agree with both), everything has its own form of awareness. In a profound sense everything is alive, aware and responsive. And everything, even that which Western scientists might consider "dead" matter, has a Higher Self with which one can consciously communicate. Unconscious communication, or subconscious telepathy, is constantly taking place between us and our environment because it is the primary way in which the world interacts with itself. An example of this would be the way that plants have been shown to respond to the pain or pleasure of other living beings nearby. As humans, however, we have the potential for conscious, deliberate telepathic communication with anything, and thus the potential for purposefully influencing our environment through non-physical means. Along with this goes the idea that there are god-selves (*aumakuas* or simply *akuas*) for groups of things as well as for individuals, and that the group essence is more than just the sum of its parts. Thus a tree has its own *aumakua*, as does the forest of which the tree is a part, the valley in which the forest lies, and so on to the very world itself—and beyond. In the old days a kahuna would ask permission from the spirit of a tree before he cut it, or from the spirit of a valley before he crossed it. He did this out of respect for the same source that lived in all of them and in order to ensure cooperation. Today a kahuna might talk to his car or his house in the same way, and use the same concept in his healing work.

As I have pointed out in other writings, the English word *spirit* covers a wide variety of phenomena which the kahunas recognize as quite different. To be brief, within this broad category the kahunas recognize thoughtforms, manifestations of energy fields, complexes appearing as separate personalities, effects of extreme telepathic or clairvoyant sensitivity, the equivalent of angels, as well as "ideas in action." In spite of popular tales and legends, kahuna philosophy does not include the idea of actual devils, demons or wandering spirits of the dead. These are seen as thoughtforms created consciously or unconsciously, or manifestations of negative complexes. Nevertheless, a kahuna might act as if such things really existed when treating a person who sincerely believes in them.

Beliefs and Reality

For the kahunas, belief is the fundamental basis for experience of any reality. The idea is that our experience is conditioned by what we believe, and we can only experience what we do believe is possible at some level of consciousness. The more firmly we believe something, the more profoundly it affects our experience. Obviously, a major task of the kahuna healer is to help people change their beliefs from unhealthy to healthy ones.

The beliefs that people hold can be divided into three types, all maintained at the same time. The first is assumption (*paulele*), a state of belief in which there are no doubts whatsoever and experience is consistent with what one believes. The second is attitude (*kuana*), beliefs which have room for doubt but which are so habitual that they continue to influence experience. The third is opinion (*mana'o*), a belief that is easily changed in the light of new knowledge. By contrast, new knowledge alone that contradicts assumptions and attitudes will rarely produce change. I will go into these beliefs and their effects on health more thoroughly in the mind/body chapter.

You create your own reality by your beliefs, say the kahunas, and the kinds of reality you create can also be classified into three categories. Western psychologists are familiar with so-called subjective and objective realities. To those, kahunas add a third, which I will call *projective*.

Subjective reality is *pono'i*, a word that refers to one's personal sense of what is right, proper, good, moral, correct, successful, useful, etc. It is the reality of judgment, and the one that has the greatest effect on health and happiness. For instance, in my personal reality, backpacking is a positive and beneficial activity, but in my wife's personal reality it is negative and painful. This is not simply a difference of opinion; it is a difference in subjective experience.

Next is objective reality, or as I prefer to call it, shared reality. The word for this is *oia'i'o*, which has meanings of substance and facts, and refers to the way things seem to be regardless of attitudes and opinions. It is the reality of appearance and interpretation, of technology and the practical dealing with the material world. The "facts" of your immediate environment allow you to eat, breathe, work, play and interact with others, and this is the reality of *oia'i'o*. This reality is most easily changed through a reinterpretation of facts, such as is often done by inventors.

The third kind of reality is *maoli*, which has the meaning of "due to vibration." This is reality which begins as subjective and becomes objectified through continued mental projection. It is a reality that you create or share in creating on purpose, bringing your desire from the level of an idea or image to the level of physical experience. It isn't something strange that only adepts can do after long years of disciplined practice. You do it every time you plan and carry out a project. Virtually the same process can be used to bring about a healing. The kahunas do not see reality as something apart from or outside of ourselves, but treat it all as part and parcel of a psychological state. The potential we have is emphasized by the fact that *maoli* can also be translated as "a state of joy."

Life and Death

The Hawaiian word for life is *ola* and the same word is used for "a means of support or income, to heal or be healed, well-being, welfare, safe, salvation, to grant life," and other similar meanings. The roots give a basic meaning of emitting or being filled with light, and the kahunas use light as a symbol for both energy and awareness. A fundamental idea behind this is that a healthy, productive and satisfying life is intimately connected with a continual increase in awareness. Two other words meaning life, *ea* and *ha*, both mean "breath" as well, that dual meaning appearing common to many ancient philosophies. In addition, these two words carry meanings associated with the movement of water; and water itself (*wai*), is also used as a symbol for life. Thus, life is perceived by the kahunas as something that flows and moves in cycles, like breath and water. In fact, a recurring phrase in legends and prayers of Hawaii, *wai ola*, can mean equally "the water of life" and "the flow of life."

From a Western point of view it seems natural to look

upon death as the opposite of life, and to expect that the kahuna word for it would refer to a stoppage of the flow. Instead, however, kahuna philosophy treats death as a continuation of life in a different direction or state. This is evident in the alternative meanings for common and poetic terms for death in Hawaiian given below:

make loa—"strong desire for something"
hiamoe loa—"desire for a long sleep"
ua makukoa'e 'oia—"life that keeps flowing"
ala ho'i ole mai—"the path of no return"
waiho na iwi—"to leave behind the bones"
moe kau a ho'oilo—"sleep time for germinating (rebirth)"
a lele nui ka mauli—"the spirit (or life) has flown"
lele ka hoaka—"the spirit (or astral body) has flown"
ha'ule—"to begin to do something"

An important problem for many philosophies is not only why death occurs, but why it occurs when it does and in the way it does. On the surface it appears illogical, without pattern or reason, but this is only because Western culture tends to look upon death as an ending, something imposed on us against our will for which we have no responsibility except in the case of suicide. The kahuna view is very different. Death is seen as part of life, as natural as the changing of seasons or the metamorphosis of a caterpillar into a butterfly. It occurs because it is part of the ongoing life process. The when and how are largely matters of personal and cultural belief. For instance, if you develop the belief that old age is a terrible thing, that you would rather die than grow old, you probably will, even if you have to subconsciously create a disease or an accident as a way to go. And if you have a deeply held belief that you can grow old gracefully, enjoyably and in full health, then you will probably be an active centenarian and pass on quietly and peacefully when you feel your life has been fulfilled. And right up until the last moment of physical life, a change in belief can change your circumstances. As I often tell my students, you have a purpose, and your Higher Self will see to it that you carry out that purpose, whether it's done in a few hours or a hundred years, whether you do it kicking and screaming all the way or having a delightful time.

The after-life is given little consideration by the kahunas because they are more concerned with the experience of the present life. In general, it is considered as a place for review of the life one has lived, for refreshment and renewal of old acquaintances, and for new experience and growth. The name for this state is *Po*, and kahunas hold that we visit it nightly in dreams when we are free from the body and also in certain trance states. We were born out of *Po*, we visit it regularly, and we shall return to it, perhaps to be born out of it again. By *we* is meant the intellect and the body (*Lono/Ku* portion of the whole self), for the Higher Self (*aumakua*) exists continually in *Po*. The English language is sometimes an awkward tool for discussing certain aspects of Huna. The impression is easily given that *Po* is a place, but that isn't accurate. It's more like a multi-dimensional state existing simultaneously and co-spatially with physical life. A rough analogy would be the TV programs that are going on in and around you right now in a form you can't normally perceive. Waking life, according to Huna, is like being attuned to a particular channel of reality in order to gain certain kinds of experience. Communication between *Po* and *Ao* (waking life) is possible because the whole person exists in both at the same time, and all that is involved is a shift in awareness. In some contexts, *Po* also means "Mind."

Reincarnation is a part of kahuna philosophy, but the concept is radically different from that of most other systems of thought because the kahuna concept of time is also radically different. Briefly, time is a form of energy vibration, like sound or light, and has frequency ranges as they do. All "times" are happening at once, but our physical senses normally restrict our awareness to a particular range we call the present. With our minds, we can transcend physical limits and be aware of those portions of our whole self that "now" exist in other times and places. The practical result of this concept is that the kahunas do not see the present life as the outcome or the effect of conditions in a "previous" life. They do not, in short, accept the idea of "karmic debt" whereby one has to pay for or make up for experiences and actions in a past life. Instead, they would say that you contain all your so-called reincarnational experiences within you at this moment as more or less latent data, and that your present life is latent data for your other lives. You affect them as much as they affect you. The relationship is more one of parallel reflection than of cause and effect, and your present belief system governs what portions of what other lives you can be aware of. You can change your beliefs by exploring, understanding and affecting "past" lives, or by exploring, understanding and affecting this one. As far as the kahunas are concerned, it is all the same thing, and what is important is bringing about the desired results.

Good and Evil

Any philosophy designed to serve as a guideline for human conduct must deal with the problem of good and evil as it appears in the world. The kahuna approach is extremely practical and simple. To begin with, there is no parallel in Huna to the notion of an evil being such as Satan, who seeks to tempt and capture the souls of men, and who can be conveniently blamed for their straying from the standards set up by other men. The kahunas consider Satan and the like as personifications of men's ideas about evil. They teach that every human being is responsible for his own actions and the results of those actions. Nor is there any concept of sinning against God, in the Western sense. God's laws are natural laws such as gravity, momentum, magnetism, etc. Such laws by their very nature cannot be "sinned" against without immediate effects. Just try to sin against the law of gravity by stepping off a cliff. "Living in sin by defying God's laws" is thus an impossibility in the kahuna view. On the other hand, this does not mean that men cannot commit evil acts.

There are three words in Hawaiian most commonly translated as *sin*, and examining them will reveal much about kahuna thinking in this area. The first word is *hala*, and its essential meaning is "to err by omission." It is the missing of the path, the failure to do something that needs to be done. Rather than a sin in the Western sense, it is actually considered to be a mistake, an error in judgment that can and ought to be rectified for the good of the individual as well as of society. Leaving the scene of an accident or not paying taxes are omissions which would fit in this category. The second type of sin is *hewa*, which is the mistake of going overboard, of doing something to excess, something which is too much and therefore not for the good of the individual and society. It, too, can and ought to be rectified. Alcoholism, reckless driving and disturbing the peace are *hewa* activities. Neither *hala* nor *hewa* are thought of as evil actions—stupid and crazy, perhaps, but not evil. The true word for evil is *'ino*, doing intentional harm to someone. The key word is intentional, the desire to harm willingly. It is more than a mistake because it is done with full understanding. This is a sin against oneself or another being, against life itself. And because intent is the key, only the individual who commits the act can actually judge what he has done, for similar acts can be carried out for dissimilar reasons. In war, for instance, people are killed by other people. But some kill for the pleasure of it, some for fear of being killed, and others to defend what is dear to them. Intent makes the difference, and the individual is his own judge in the ethical sense.

Using the word *society* to cover any kind of group, the kahunas recognize that a society can make any rules or laws or ethical standards that it wishes and devise any punishments for disobeying those that it deems appropriate. At the same time, an individual in that society has the right to obey those laws and receive the benefits of the society, or break them and take the consequences. A society can even set up what it considers moral laws, but they remain the laws of that particular society and are not necessarily adequate for universal application. Regardless, an individual who believes that breaking the laws of his society is a sin will find some way to punish himself even if the society doesn't, usually through sickness or accident. But aside from what a society may or may not do about a person who breaks its laws, the final judge is one's personal god-self. The only universal sin is violence to life. That includes intentional harm of any sort, and is as applicable to plants, animals or the earth itself as it is to human beings.

Love and Emotions

Max Long formulated a Huna "commandment" which he stated as "No Harm." Among kahunas, however, that principle is stated more positively as a call to love. There are no commandments in Huna. Instead, there is logic, in the sense of a necessary connection between events. If you commit violence, you will receive violence. If you love, you will be loved. This has nothing to do with commandments; it is the nature of life. In line with the kahuna view that experience follows thought and that everything is part of a whole, it follows that you cannot commit violence without first feeling violent about yourself; you cannot hate others without first hating yourself; and you cannot truly love without first loving yourself. As WK has said, "If you don't have it in you, you can't give it out." Love is oriented toward growth and development, while violence is restrictive and repressive. The call to love, then, is very practical. If you want to grow and develop and enjoy life, practice love. And to the degree that you practice it, necessarily starting with yourself, to that same degree you will grow and develop and enjoy.

In order to practice love, though, you have to understand what it is. For many people in Western culture it seems to be a kind of sickness or a form of emotional trauma, to judge from their descriptions of it. The Hawaiian word for love is *aloha*, which most tourists to Honolulu know also means "Hello" and "Goodbye." But *aloha* is used for those greetings precisely because it does mean love, for the best way to greet or take leave of people is with love. Now what is love? The word itself gives the answer. According to the roots, it means "to grow and thrive joyously together," "to share the experience of life," and "to be happy with." Love is a way of acting toward and with others, and a way of feeling about yourself and others. The way of acting is always a healing one, encouraging the object of love to thrive and grow; the way of feeling is always a happy and joyful one. You could say, then, that to love is to heal, and to heal is to love. Of course, anything can be *called* love, but the real test is whether it encourages growth and happiness.

Emotions are seen by the kahunas as an excitement or movement of energy through the body, and all the Hawaiian words relating to emotions reflect this idea, generally with the use of water imagery like waves or spray or water flowing in some way. The specific name given to a particular emotion depends on the thoughts that accompany it. In terms of pure sensation, you can't tell the difference between anger and enthusiasm, or anxiety and excited anticipation. The stimulation of emotional flow can come from your thoughts or an outside event, but in any case the thoughts are what perpetuate the emotion, and a change of thinking can change the emotions you experience.

Relativity

The concept of relativity is very important in kahuna philosophy, especially in regard to healing. The Huna idea is quite similar to the yin/yang concept of the Chinese, i.e., everything is relative to something else. Nothing can be described or experienced except in relation to something else because there are no absolutes in the world of our perception. This is a logical extension of a basic kahuna assumption that God or the Godhead is infinite, and infinite means unlimited. From this we can get the following proposition:

> God is infinite;
> Therefore God is all truth;
> Therefore truth is infinite;
> Therefore everything that is, is true.

Since man cannot perceive infinity, he can never perceive more than a portion of the truth, and that portion depends entirely on his system of beliefs. As man's beliefs change, so does his truth, and therefore his experience. The perception of truth, then, is relative to your state of mind, so all that you can experience at any given time is a relative truth. This is effectively brought out in the language of Huna because most of the "code" words contain relative meanings. The word *sacred* (*la'a*) also means "cursed and defiled," and even the word *aloha*, so strongly associated with reaching out, making contact and sharing, has additional root meanings of avoiding and withholding. The idea behind these paradoxical translations is that the meaning depends on the circumstances. Meaning can only be understood in relation to its environment. Therefore, the words only make full sense in context.

In a broader sense, any portion of the universe is what it appears to be only in relation to some other part with which it can be compared. There are no absolutes; there is no meaning without relationships; everything is not only interacting but interdependent. The kahunas use this idea to help give a person a powerfully secure sense of significance, while at the same time teaching him that to heal himself is to heal the world, and to heal the world is to heal himself. This is not a loss of individuality, but an understanding that individuality itself is a relationship with the environment.

The general philosophical ideas briefly presented above form the basis for the kahuna practices to be described in the following chapters.

 CHAPTER 3

Psychic Practices

In legends, historical narratives and travelers' anecdotes, many tales are told of psychic practices carried out by the kahunas of Hawaii, practices which are still noted to this day and which are an essential part of kahuna healing methods. Although plenty of controversy remains, this is not the place to try to prove the existence of psychic abilities. In this chapter I will concentrate on the kahuna explanation and use of them.

Levels of Awareness

As described in the previous chapter, the kahunas recognize several ways of perceiving reality, and they also use several levels of awareness in carrying out their practices, each with its own set of rules or framework of beliefs. This follows the philosophical concept that we live in a multidimensional universe, and that we can achieve different effects and experiences by shifting our focus from one dimension or level to another. These levels are thought to coexist, so that moving from one to another merely involves a shift in attention. It could be likened to living in a one-room apartment which can be used for sleeping, dining, reading or creative work. As we do one or another, the room hasn't changed at all, just the use of it and our perception of it. WK likes to divide these levels into four different types. However, the kahunas see all categorizations or divisions of any kind as potentially useful but always arbitrary. Separateness is just a handy illusion. So kahunas feel free to develop any kind of explanatory framework that serves their purposes. With that in mind, here are WK's four levels:

First Level: Physical (*Ike Papakahi*)

This is the level of what could be termed *gross physical experience*. It refers to the ordinary everyday realm that we know and work with through sight, sound, touch, taste, and smell and feeling. This level is not unreal, but it's a level of only partial awareness. It is a pragmatic level in which houses can be built, food can be eaten, and where people can relate to each other with a semblance of independence. Its dominant characteristic is a sense of objective experience, of a separateness between people, objects and events.

Second Level: Psychic (*Ike Papalua*)

This is the level of most psychic experience. In this state, objective experience is not as sharply defined because you can communicate with your environment and influence it in ways that would not be possible in strictly first level action. Subjectivity becomes more important, but it is used as a means of acting on the outer world. From here you can use mental techniques to create objective events.

Third Level: Relational (*Ike Papakolu*)

This is a state of interrelatedness or relativity. Time, space, matter, energy, humans, plants, animals all become relative concepts which are constantly interacting and which have no meaning except in relation to each other. While the first two states are primarily action oriented, this one and the next are more information oriented. For instance, an adept kahuna might use this state to learn the true nature of a person's illness, shift to the second state to perform a psychic healing, and shift again to the first to give a massage or herbal remedy or to do a ritual to impress the patient.

Fourth Level: Mystical (*Ike Papakauna*)

This is a state of mystical awareness of the oneness of the universe. Some writers have called it *cosmic consciousness*, and while the experience of it can alter the way a person looks at life and how he decides to act thereafter, it is a purely subjective state and cannot be used in any "practical" way. As an example, if a kahuna, without any means of physical protection, were faced with a man-eating lion, he could use the second level to telepathically influence the lion to leave him alone, and he could shift to third level to determine why he allowed himself to get into such a situation and learn how to change this thinking so as not to do it again. If he were to shift to this fourth level he would understand that he and the lion were united in the great scheme of things and that whatever happened would be right and good in the eyes of the universe. However, if he relied on that state alone, he would probably be eaten.

Mind, Energy and Matter

In his search for the knowledge of the kahunas, Max

Long said he was directed to look for three factors: a form of consciousness (*no'ono'o*), a form of force (*mana*), and a form of substance (*aka*). As all three are essential to kahuna psychic practices, a brief explanation of each is required.

In this context consciousness (*no'ono'o*) is thought in the form of imagination, and it has two aspects. One is "eyes of the subconscious" (*makaku*), imagination based on current beliefs. It can manifest as memory images, dreams, habitual or spontaneous daydreams, and even pictured worries or anticipations. This aspect is used in psychic information gathering (imagination is not just fantasy), and it is usually called "tuning in" by psychics. The second aspect (*laulele*) has root meanings of forming an embryonic pattern and also of spreading and flying outward. This is imagination consciously willed and directed, the kind an architect might use before setting his ideas down on paper. With *laulele* the kahuna establishes a mental pattern for what he desires to achieve, which fits in with the philosophical idea of projective reality. This idea is contained in the root *'ono* of *no'ono'o*, which means "to crave, to desire to achieve something." The idea intended is that of emotionally powered, strongly directed will. Of the many Hawaiian equivalents for the English word *desire*, only *'ono* carries the idea of intent toward achieving something. *No'ono'o*, then, is purposeful creative imagination.

For the kahuna, the real key to psychic work is psychic force or divine power (*mana*). This refers to power of any kind, but especially confidence and energy. As energy, it is the life force that permeates the universe, which is highly concentrated in living things. It can be accumulated, focused and transferred from one person or object to another. *Mana* seems to have many of the characteristics of electricity, magnetism and gravity, and the kahunas view these as variations of it.

The effectiveness of all psychic practices is determined by its abundance or scarcity. Therefore, a great deal of attention is paid to learning how to consciously increase the available supply. One way is by using conscious imagination or visualization, imagining that the *mana* is increasing—as indeed it does. When kahuna practices of this nature are carried out, you can actually feel physical sensations in the body such as currents, tingling or heat, all signs of increased *mana* flow. Another way is to practice various forms of specialized breathing and exercise, similar to what a yogi might use. This is based on the idea that *mana* is also in the air and can be pulled in more abundantly by consciously controlled breathing. Certain foods thought to have particularly strong concentrations of *mana* may be eaten, and special objects believed to have large amounts of *mana* might be handled in various ways. Sound in the form of songs, chants and music can be used as well. By far the most common practice, however, is the conscious building up of emotion. To the kahunas, emotion is more than just feeling; it is the movement of *mana* in the body accompanied by a specific thought. Strong emotion is equated with the presence of a great concentration of *mana*. The proficient kahuna is expected to be a master of emotions, able to generate them, direct them and dissipate them at will. Virtually all the descriptive words used in Huna for psychic practices contain roots that clearly indicate the use of emotion in carrying them out. Note this, however: the more *mana*-as-confidence you have, the less *mana*-as-energy you need; and the less *mana*-as-confidence you have, the more *mana*-as-energy you need.

Aka is the basic "stuff" of the physical universe, out of which every material manifestation is formed. The word has meanings of "luminous, transparent, shadow, reflection, mirror, essence." *Aka* acts like a mirror to reflect patterns of thought on both the psychic and physical levels. Compared to the realm of pure thought, it is a mere shadow. The kahunas believe that this "stuff" can be formed and shaped by conscious and unconscious thought, and that it acts as a container for *mana*. The more *mana* it contains, the more dense it appears. Some forms of *aka* are known to psychics as etheric or astral matter, and under certain conditions in the psychic state of awareness it appears as luminously transparent. The reflective characteristics of this stuff are what enable a kahuna healer to change conditions by changing thinking.

Symbology

In teaching and practicing their psychic cráfts, the kahunas make great use of metaphorical symbols and tools. Unlike some Western occultists who may attribute inherent magical properties to the physical tools of their trade, the kahunas are well aware that the primary purpose of such tools is to stimulate the production of *mana* by the subconscious, and to direct its flow in a given direction by the conscious mind. Of course, any particular object might be infused with an extra supply of *mana*, which could make it a more effective stimulant, but the tools used by the kahunas were honored more for the double meaning of their names than for any natural effectiveness they might have.

For instance, a traditional tool used in many ancient kahuna rituals was a narcotic drink made from *awa* (kava) root. The reasoning behind this was that the word *aka* means an "unpleasant or tragic experience and also a channel or passage through a reef into a peaceful harbor." In offering up the *awa* to the gods, the kahuna was actually performing a ritual to convince the subconscious that bitter experiences were being replaced by inner peace. Another tool still used in Hawaii for various practices, often protective, is the *ki* (ti) leaf, because other meanings for *ki* include "force, attack, bind, and to take away."

Animals, plants, flowers, fishes, birds, stones and other objects were all utilized according to various meanings contained in their names, quite apart from their use as an extra source of *mana* or for any chemical or nutritional characteristics. The kahunas know that the real power of a word rests in its psychological significance. Sound alone can stimulate a flow of *mana*, but sound formed into a word with psychological impact has a much greater effect.

In teaching and learning, it is often useful to apply metaphors. In the teaching of electrical theory, for example, a student might be told that electricity is like water flowing through a pipe, with the flow like the current, the pressure like the voltage, and the friction against the pipe like the resistance. Kahunas also use metaphors in a similar way to explain the different aspects of the concepts they teach. Following are some of the metaphors used by Hawaiian kahunas to describe the effects and actions of the three prime factors of imaginative thought, energy or power, and matter:

> Thoughts—bundles, clusters, seeds, nets, webs, any piercing instruments, clubs, sprouts and young animals, fishes and flowers.

Power—water, rain, mist and fog, waves and swells, fire, food, branches or limbs, and colors (especially red).

Matter (etheric)—a bridge, an arch or arc, a rainbow, a cave or cavern, rope, thread or cord, shadows, an embryo, joints of the body, hooks and clouds.

With such symbolism the kahunas are able to teach their concepts in a way that students can easily relate to the natural world.

Categories of Psychic Powers

Classifying the psychic practices of the kahunas presents somewhat of a problem because the Western categories are based on rather different assumptions. For the kahunas, all psychic practices are only variations on one basic process which utilizes thought, energy and etheric matter, either to communicate, to change conditions, or to do both at once. Also, such practices are believed by them to involve extensions of our existing senses, not "extra" ones. Nevertheless, for the purpose of discussion I will divide kahuna psychic practices into the areas of telepathy, clairvoyance, precognition and psychokinesis. You must understand, however, that these are categories of function, not nature, and that in actual practice they overlap. The kahuna interpretation of them differs from the Western in many respects.

Telepathy (*Una*)

In its strictest kahuna usage, *una* (telepathy) is the transmission of thoughts or ideas by an action of mind and psychic energy. It refers only to sending, not receiving, and it refers only to intentional telepathy. The kahunas believe that mental communication is a natural function of all human beings, and that it is in constant operation in spite of people's limited awareness of it. This kind of unconscious communication is called *ike hanau*, which may be translated as "instinct." *Una* differs in that it is willfully applied, and the process is quite simple. You focus your attention on the person you want to make contact with, build up a surplus of *mana*, hold clearly in mind the thought you want to transmit, and will it on its way. However, practical effectiveness is only achieved with disciplined practice and a thorough knowledge of the nature of mind, energy and matter. In this it is no different from any other skill which requires practice and knowledge. In healing, a kahuna will use intentional telepathy to transmit positive healing suggestions to the patient, in addition to whatever other techniques he might use. The kahunas teach that this ability is not affected by distance, but when transmitting to a patient who is out of sight it becomes even more important to hold a clear image of him. In the olden days bits of personal belongings were used when available, to aid concentration; nowadays a kahuna might use a signature or a photograph.

Clairvoyance (*Kilo/Nana Ao*)

The word *clairvoyance* covers two distinct kinds of phenomena: the ability to receive information mentally (*kilo*); and the ability to see auras and free-standing energy forms (*nana ao*).

Mental reception includes the Western idea of telepathic receiving and the technique known as "psychometry," a process whereby one obtains information about people and events from an object somehow related to them. Also included are those forms of clairvoyance in which an intermediary tool is used, such as scrying (crystal ball gazing), card reading and the interpretation of omens. All of these use the same basic technique for achieving a state of mental communication (*ike papalua*) through various concentration and dissociation exercises: focusing the mind on the intended source of information; being alert to the input in the form of images, sensations and feelings during the period of focus; translating that input into meaningful output. When applied to healing, these practices are used primarily for diagnosing the mental and attitudinal causes of illness and for locating the areas of tension in the body. You can realize the problem of using Western categories when the kahunas see no difference between receiving information telepathically from a human or clairvoyantly from a rock.

WK says that the term *nana ao* refers to the ability to see such things as auras, energy fields and etheric or astral bodies, although the phrase is translated in the Hawaiian dictionary as "cloud interpretation" (in the sense of treating the shapes of clouds in the sky as omens). I have demonstrated in hundreds of cases that anyone can see auras and energy fields if they know what to look for and how to look, but most people are never told they can. *Nana ao*, however, includes the ability to interpret what you see. The kahunas who practice this for healing use it to determine tension areas in the body. They also assess emotional states by visual interpretation of the colors they see and/or areas of relative brightness and darkness. As a variation, some kahunas use the sense of touch instead of visual interpretation, and this is called *haha*. In such a case, the kahuna may run his hands over the body of the patient or a few inches above the skin and sense areas of "smoothness" or "roughness," with the latter indicating problem areas. A kahuna practicing clairvoyant vision will seldom rely on it alone, but will include telepathy as part of the process.

Precognition (*Wanana*)

Precognition—the art of divination—is a concept that baffles and frustrates scientists and philosophers alike. Yet, the weight of evidence demonstrates that it is apparently possible to see into the future and have foreknowledge of coming events, even though no one has ever been found to be one hundred percent accurate. In fact, the inaccuracy of psychic forecasting has some researchers even more baffled. The question naturally arises as to why some forecasts are highly accurate, some partially so, and others not at all, even when given by the same person.

Divination, or precognition, is a regular kahuna practice, and all adept kahunas use it to some degree. Since it is included as part of kahuna training, it should not be surprising that the language roots contain definite information as to the nature of time and precognition. The main word for divination, *wanana*, means "to observe the patterns of time."

Our normal and psychic senses tell us that the past consists of events which have occurred, and the future consists of events which have not yet occurred. It seems reasonable to assume, then, that the present consists of events which are occurring and being perceived. The idea of present time, however, poses a problem to those who have been led into thinking of past and future as objective concepts. Some Eastern philosophies claim that the present is an illusion because time is a continuous flow from past into future. Certain Western scientists more or less agree by saying that, because it can't be objectively measured, the present is merely an interface between past and future. In contrast, the kahuna view of the present is that it involves the span of events which you are in the process of perceiving and with which you can interact. One phrase used to designate the present is *i keia manawa*, meaning "in this flow of mana," or "in this space/time authority." This gives a broader view of the present which is more in line with our perceptions.

The most significant word for the past is *wa'ae'oia*, which means "the period of enduring agreement." This reflects the idea that the past is what we remember it to be and what we agree that it is, as well as memories existing in the present. We get a closer glimpse of the kahuna ideas underlying divination in the phrase for *future, ka wa mahope.* Outwardly, it means "the time that comes after," but *mahope* also means "result, consequence," indicating the kahuna teaching that the future is a result of what goes on in the present. Another word for the present, *'ano*, contains this idea as well. Its alternate meanings are "seed, offspring." The kahunas teach that the present is the fruit of the past, and the seed of the future. Therefore, by carefully examining the present, one can predict the future. There is no need to bypass or transcend time, a doubtful possibility in any case. The future grows out of what is happening now.

However, this does not imply any kind of predetermination, because the present moment is dynamic, flowing, not static. Every change of thought or action introduces new variables that can change the course of the future, and one of the variables is the forecaster himself. The kahunas know that even expressing a forecast can affect the future. Nearly all the Huna words dealing with prophecy contain allusions to this. And the kahunas also know that the more information you have about the present, the more accurate your forecasts can be. Therefore, they don't limit their information to what is available physically, but open up their minds telepathically and clairvoyantly to gather information from as many sources as possible.

Divination, then, consists of expanding your awareness to include unseen aspects of the present moment as well as ordinary knowledge, and then drawing conclusions as to what the most likely result will be at any given future time. This psychic information gathering is usually a subconscious process, that is, the mass of information doesn't have to be made available to the conscious mind. Given the order to gather information, the subconscious of the diviner makes a kind of "probability estimate" of the future and presents this to the conscious mind in the form of words or images. The kahunas say that this is the process employed by all psychic forecasters, whether they are aware of it or not. The most accurate predicting concerns the near future or those events whose past "seeds" have been abundantly sown, because there is less opportunity for new variables to be introduced. The real skill of the kahuna diviner lies in his ability to receive and interpret information without prejudice. To the extent he can do this, his predictions will be as accurate as possible in a world of infinite potential. (The latter ability is lacking in many modern seers who predict what they wish would happen, rather than what is probable.)

When divination is used in a healing context, it is done to check the potential course of an illness and the potential outcome of various treatment methods. Based on this information, the kahuna will either go ahead with what he planned or modify it. He will use the same information to give advice to the patient for self-treatment and direction.

The idea of consciously influencing the future is inextricably wound up with kahuna divination. Once the kahuna has seen the probable results of today's thoughts and action, he may take steps to change those thoughts and actions, i.e., to purposely introduce new variables so as to change the probable outcome. It is here that divination merges with psychokinesis, in kahuna terms.

Psychokinesis (*Kalakupua*)

Western researchers define psychokinesis as "the placing of an object in motion by volition alone," but this limited definition does not suit the kahunas. In the first place, they teach that volition alone (*'ono*) can accomplish nothing. Also required are imagination (*no'ono'o*) to provide the pattern for the movement, energy (*mana*) to provide the power, and a reactive medium (*aka*) through which the power can work. Without these, even the most intense volition will not be effective. As a matter of fact, the existence of unconscious psychokinesis, as in poltergeist activity, would seem to rule out volition as being necessary at all. In the second place, under the category of psychokinesis the kahunas would include all practices in which mind-directed *mana* is used to produce effects without direct physical intervention. Their reasoning is that such varied activities as the nonphysical movement of objects, psychic healing, psychic weather control and changing the future are all achieved by the same process. It is only the intent that differs. As the kahunas believe that the physical world is a reflection of thought, they would consider that all changes in conditions are brought about by psychokinesis, using their extended interpretation, and that this is a natural process employed unconsciously by everyone in greater or lesser degrees.

For consciously controlled psychokinesis, WK gave me the word *kalakupua*, which the early missionaries translated as *magic*. An inner meaning of this word based on the roots would be "to release one's power and transform desires into completed action." The word *kupua* is a synonym for *mana* or one possessing *mana*, and its roots contain many references to accomplishing things through thought, particularly persistent thought.

Psychokinetic Destruction (*Ana-ana*)

Although this book is concerned with kahuna healing, it would not be complete without a clear explanation of how others can be harmed through the same process. The kahunas teach that the only difference between psychokinetic healing and psychokinetic destruction is the intent of the practitioner, for the process used for each is virtually the same, and the end result is determined by the kinds of thoughts and emotions brought into play. This exposé is not intended to frighten nor to give a working method to those who might attempt to abuse their psychic abilities. Its purpose is to clarify a long misunderstood and rare process so you can see that there is less to be afraid of than you might have thought.

Tales of sorcerers able to cause harm to their victims at a distance can be found in practically every culture. When I lived in West Africa this was a common fear among the people there, and some of these sorcerers made a living by blackmailing victims with a kind of protection racket. In Hawaii to this day *ana-ana* sorcerers are feared because they might use the dreaded "death prayer" on someone who breaks an ancient *kapu* or just irritates the sorcerer. Western "experts" who have little or no experience with this phenomenon usually pass it off as mere superstition based on the victim's fear. Unfortunately, in Hawaii the practice has become associated with kahunas in general. Even Max Long, that untiring researcher of Huna lore, thought that the kahunas at one time used the death prayer to punish wrongdoers. The fact is that only renegade kahunas and independent, perverted sorcerers ever resorted to this practice.

It would be a serious error to consider telepathic destruction as merely superstition based on fear alone. Successful experiments with the telepathic transmission of ideas, emotions and directives done by modern researchers in parapsychology clearly provide a basis for the acceptance of the concept, distasteful though it may be. The term *ana-ana*, as used in Hawaiian, implies doing something to excess according to plan, and is used generically to cover all practices which could be called "black magic," but especially the so-called death prayer. Max Long recorded the following death prayer, given as an order to the "god" Lono. This translation only makes sense in the context of alternate meanings of the words themselves and when you understand kahuna thinking about the nature of the mind.

> O Lono
> Listen to my voice.
> This is the plan:
> Rush upon _____ and enter;
> Enter and curl up;
> Curl up and straighten out.[4]

The prayer did double duty as a stimulus to the subconscious of the practitioner and as a strong telepathic suggestion to the victim. Of course, the complete process involves much more than the simple recitation of a prayer.

The *ana-ana* practitioner first makes mental contact with the intended victim. This may be done directly by conjuring up an image of the victim in the practitioner's mind or, more commonly, by handling something belonging to the victim. The latter technique is based on the idea that the etheric pattern of an individual leaves an invisible and lasting impression on the energy field of whatever objects he contacts. This impression is often symbolized in Huna as a sticky thread that connects the object and the person. A further idea is that this impression can be "read" by a skilled psychic and also used to make mental contact with the person who handled it. It was for this reason that the chiefs of old Hawaii took great pains to make sure that their hair trimmings, nail parings, excreta and even their bones after death were all carefully hidden or disposed of so that no destructive sorcerer could obtain them. This, however, was superstition, because a trained psychic doesn't need anything physical to make such contact, although such objects are often used because they make concentration easier.

The victim's fears and guilts form the basis of the psychic "hook" that the practitioner establishes through telepathic transmission of thought and emotion, and the success of *ana-ana* is based on the exaggeration and distortion of these. The more fears and guilts dominate his or her thoughts, the more quickly the victim succumbs.

Since the intent of the *ana-ana* sorcerer is not to prove a method but to achieve an end, any technique that will hasten the process is also used. Thus, if a victim knows that *ana-ana* is being worked on him, this acts as a strong suggestion to weaken his resistance. In fact, in some cases this is all the sorcerer has to do, because the actual work of destruction will be carried out by the victim himself, and this has given rise to the Western belief that nothing more is involved. At other times, the practitioner may use a technique by which an object is "charged" with an emotionally laden thought conforming to the victim's fears or guilts and placed in his vicinity, preferably in his hands. This kind of object, when used for this purpose, is called "bait" (*manu*). It can also affect innocent bystanders who have some degree of the same fears and guilts suffered by the victim.

The *ana-ana* sorcerer may use trickery, suggestion, rumors, poison or anything else to get his victim to succumb. But the psychic part of the process is virtually identical to that used by healing kahunas for distant healing. The main differences are the intent, the nature of the thoughts and emotions used, and the fact that the strengths of the receiver are emphasized, rather than the fears and guilts.

Fortunately for mankind, there are three natural factors that diminish the dangers of destructive sorcery. First is the instinct for survival that helps to protect everyone to some extent from the effects of negative thoughts and emotions. If this weren't true the earth would have been depopulated a long time ago. Second is the fact that *ana-ana* sorcery requires a great deal of skill and training, and there are very few who would willingly undergo it since it involves an extremely distasteful process of dehumanization. Third is the fact that destructive sorcerers in any culture are notoriously short-lived because the powerful negative emotions they must generate wreak havoc on their own minds and bodies. In spite of popular tales and legends, there are no elderly evil sorcerers. They just look old. A fourth important factor is that those who practice the various forms of *ana-ana* and even the milder forms like "love magic" (*hana aloha*) have never been allowed to do so with impunity.

Some healing kahunas have specialized in certain ways of protecting the weak from harmful influence, and I will discuss a few of these methods next.

Counter-Sorcery

There are three broad categories of techniques used in kahuna counter-sorcery. The most commonly used because of its general effectiveness is *pale*. The roots refer to a barrier against waves, indicating protection against waves of emotion used in *ana-ana* or even unconsciously transmitted emotions. In its simplest form, *pale* is the imagining of an encircling shield of white light (*la'a kea*) accompanied by strong positive emotions and suggestions of strength and protection. *Pale* is most effective when the individual is taught to use it on his own and when he believes in its effectiveness. However, as long as there is not active disbelief, a complete belief is not necessary. If you practice this yourself, you need never worry about negative thoughts and emotions coming from someone else, whether deliberate or unconscious.

Another category of counter-sorcery methods, mainly used by the Emotionals of the Order of Ku, retains a kind of "eye for an eye" philosophy. All of these techniques (*kuni, ho'i-ho'i* and *'a'e*) have to do with inflicting destruction upon the sorcerer by the same means used on the victim. In a story related to Max Long, the former curator of the Bishop Museum in Hawaii used a sending-back technique to protect his young porter and kill the offending sorcerer.

The third technique used in counter-sorcery, primarily by the Orders of Lono and Kane (Intellectuals and Intuitionists) is *kala*, which among other things means "to free one from evil influence." Its basis is the release of the victim from the fears and guilts themselves, the "undoing of the hooks." In essence, it is a form of psychotherapy applicable to *ana-ana* sorcery as well as the elimination of negative complexes. I would remind you that the true kahunas do not really believe in possession by evil spirits in the Western sense, whether sent by a sorcerer or not. This is clearly evident in the root meanings of the word for exorcism, *mahiki*, which indicates a peeling away of negative beliefs from the past.

Psychic Abilities Are Natural

Psychic abilities, according to the kahunas, are a natural part of being human. Everyone uses them on a daily basis, and without them we could not survive. Telepathic communication with friends and strangers, clairvoyant impressions from one's surroundings, divinatory hunches and dreams about the future, and psychokinetic influence of events all occur spontaneously in every man, woman and child. Here in the West the cultural bias of modern society has largely suppressed our awareness of these happenings, unless they shock or frighten us. A few individuals who are generally called *psychics* (the old word *sensitives* is perhaps more accurate) have, for various reasons, not suppressed this kind of awareness, and more or less openly make use of it. But they seldom have much understanding or control over what they are doing. A review of the lives of such people does show, however, that spiritual, mental, emotional or physical perfection are certainly not requirements for the achievement of psychic abilities. That is because these are inherent in all of us, not special gifts from a capricious god or qualities we lack that must be obtained. All that we have to obtain is skill in their use.

Kahunas are ordinary men and women who have been trained to develop abilities they already have, to understand what they are doing, and to control psychic practices at will. As in every human endeavor, some are more skilled in certain areas than others, and some prefer certain practices to others, but all kahunas undergo the same basic training and preparation. Regardless of the orientation of the individual, each kahuna learns four areas which are used as a framework for further development. The keywords for these areas are the same as those used for the philosophy in general (*ike, makia, kala* and *manawa*).

Awareness (Ike). This has to do with expanding awareness of your own thoughts, feelings, beliefs and behavior; awareness of these in other people; awareness of the seen and unseen environment.

Concentration (Makia). This includes not only learning concentration, but also the manipulation of imagination and emotion.

Releasing (Kala). This is a process of freeing yourself from limiting ideas and beliefs; of releasing your inner resources of energy and ability; of learning to help others do the same.

Directing (Manawa). This area deals with learning how to direct a continuous flow of *mana* to achieve a specific purpose.

The use of psychic powers is fundamental to the kahuna way of life. In their belief, mankind can never reach its full potential unless these powers are consciously used and developed.

 CHAPTER 4

The Mind/Body Approach

The whole kahuna approach to mind/body interrelationships is based on particular interpretations of three
concepts: mind, energy and matter. Western philosophy
and science have always been fascinated by possible
relations among these three, but until quite recently the
prevailing view has been that the mind and body are
quite separate entities. Great inroads have been made on
this dualistic outlook with the increasing realization of
the role that emotions play in physical illness, but a true
mind/body approach such as the kahunas use is still considered quite radical among the majority of health
practitioners. Radical it may be, but it is highly effective
and absolutely essential to the practice of kahuna healing. Even today the modern Hawaiian phrase "hang
loose" is a folk therapy reference to the kahuna idea that
unhappiness and physical illness are directly related to
mental attitudes that produce or increase tension.
Ancient Hawaiians had to deal with the hardships of war,
social disruption and food production, and modern ones

have to deal with social discrimination and the pressures of a technological civilization. Now, as then, "hanging loose" helps to bring mind and body into balance.

In this chapter I will discuss in more detail how the kahunas view the mind and its effects on health and behavior; biological energy flow; the nature and formation of complexes; and the factor of "ecological feedback." Along the way I will include comparative comments from Western psychologists and others.

In kahuna teaching, as explained, the mind has three aspects, termed *kane, ku,* and *lono.* Three alternatives are, respectively, *aumakua, unihipili* and *uhane.* These three interact intimately with the body, *kino.*

The Higher Self (*Kane/Aumakua*)

In modern psychology the equivalent to this aspect of the self would be that of an "oversoul" or the "superconscious." Although few systems of modern psychology concern themselves with such an idea, one which does is the psychosynthesis model of Roberto Assagioli, who says:

> What distinguishes psychosynthesis from many other attempts at psychological understanding is the position that we take as to the existence of a spiritual Self and of a superconscious, which are as basic as the instinctive energies described so well by Freud.[5]

He then goes on to make a distinction, with which the kahunas would agree, between the superconscious and mere high states of awareness.

The kahunas liken the role of the Higher Self to that of a teacher and a creative artist. As a teacher, it is considered to be the source of all knowledge of which you might ever have need or desire. Thus, in any particular

81

stage or circumstance of life, you have access to the knowledge of what to do to achieve a given end and how to do it. This knowledge may be presented through dreams, visions, inspirations, hunches, or through contacts which you have with people and objects in the physical world. Since this knowledge is also made available through a form of telepathy, it becomes possible to seek it out consciously by altering your state of awareness. Assagioli prescribes a kahuna-like technique for this using specific symbols, and tells his patient that "there is a wise teacher within him, his spiritual Self who already knows his problem, his crisis, his perplexity."[6] A kahuna could not have put it better.

Huna teaches that the god-self never seeks to force a certain way of thinking or acting upon the individual conscious mind. In its role as teacher it is a dispenser of information and no more. This means that it does not tell you what you should do, only what you can do. The respect for freedom of conscious choice is always maintained because that is part of the purpose for your existence here. According to the kahunas, then, if you expect a guiding inner voice to make your decisions for you, you will end up listening to your own beliefs and habits of thought, or the thoughts of others no wiser than you. The kahunas instruct students to beware of inner voices that attempt to command thought and action, for these are not from the Higher Self. In most cases they are merely personified complexes, which will be discussed further on. Assagioli recognizes the teaching role when he says that the purpose of contact with one's Higher Self is the practical one of "increased creativity, of increased ability to give of one's self to some chosen field."[7] The mystic experience, that is, the subjectively joyful experience of uniting with a greater aspect of yourself (the superconscious), is not recommended as an end in itself, either by the kahunas or the practitioners of psychosynthesis. The kahunas would agree wholeheartedly with Assagioli's statement that from such an experience the "subject has to draw the fire, the enthusiasm and incentive to come back into the world and serve God and his fellow men."[8]

In its creative role, say the kahunas, the god-self forms and sustains the physical body during the life of the individual, and also forms the individual's experience of physical reality. To do this it uses both a "group pattern" and a "personal pattern." The group pattern consists of the basic laws of nature, unlimited by cultural opinion as to what those laws are. It is like a general agreement reached by all the human Higher Selves (called the *po'e aumakua* as a group) as to what the basic constraints of physical reality shall be, such as the operation of gravity, light, electromagnetism, etc. The personal pattern is composed of the beliefs and attitudes of the individual, including those cultural opinions accepted as fact, which the god-self uses to form the subjective experience of events and circumstances.

From the kahuna point of view, this idea has practical value. While you cannot change the course of the seasons, you can change the course of events you personally experience during those seasons by altering your thinking. The idea of changing your thinking in order to alter events is not entirely novel to Western thinking, but it does go beyond traditional psychoanalytic thought which, according to Freud, aims at altering thinking in order to change *reactions* to circumstances. Maxwell Maltz, M.D., author of *Psycho-Cybernetics*, spends considerable space describing how altered thinking leads to changed circumstances;

Assagioli lists several psychological laws that he says govern this concept; Dr. Irving Oyle, author of *The Healing Mind*, is convinced that ideas can make us ill or cure us; eminent psychiatrist and hypnotherapist Dr. William S. Kroger has said that "whenever attention is concentrated on an idea over and over again, it spontaneously tends to realize itself."[9] But it is clear from a thorough reading in what might be called the "new psychologies" that the writers are thinking in terms of thought affecting behavior, and that it is the behavioral changes that lead to changed circumstances.

The kahuna concept is decidedly different. Kristin Zambucka, an author with a clear knowledge of Huna, has written that "It is only through our consciousness that God can enter this world. He then translates into our human experience."[10] God, in this context, refers to the god-self (*aumakua*). The kahunas teach that ideas *generate* circumstances, not merely condition our experience of them. As you will see, this has a profound influence on their healing methods.

According to kahuna teaching, the Higher Self creates the conditions of life brought about by personal beliefs and within the general constraints of physical reality. A god-self will interfere with events brought about by personal belief patterns only when such patterns are leading to an imminent death, injury or situation which does not fit in with the overall life purpose. Then you may experience a "miraculous" avoidance or resolution of the situation and, in a sense, be given another chance.

I feel this is the explanation for a remarkable incident that happened in Africa when I was on my way back from a safari in the Sahara. I was in the front passenger seat of my Land Rover. Two other riders were in back and my driver was at the wheel. It was night and we were on a two-lane road behind a semi that was going down the middle. My driver decided to pass by driving half on the shoulder and there we were, doing about fifty miles an hour, when the headlights showed the abutment of a one-lane bridge. On the left was a long drop to a river; on the right was the semi already starting to cross the bridge. My driver swung the wheel to the right, there was a bump, and then we were across the bridge, careening through a field till we crashed into a tree. A back door had come off and the other passengers had fallen out, but not one of us had a scratch. The semi stopped and in the *middle* of the trailer was a slight dent that matched in height and paint a scratch on the right rear roof edge of the Rover. All the indications were that we had to have crossed the bridge at the same time as the semi. On taking measurements, however, we found that the semi only cleared the bridge by three feet on each side. It is a kahuna belief that such "miracles" only happen if such a possibility lies within the beliefs of the individuals involved.

Conscious Mind (*Lono*)

The *lono* mind or self is roughly analagous to the "conscious mind" in psychology. It is that aspect of mind which focuses on physical reality, analyzes it, integrates it, and forms beliefs, attitudes and opinions about it. It is a receiver of subtle and gross information from various sources and a director of action. How well it directs, of course, depends on the beliefs it has accepted. So long as it believes itself to be powerless, it will act according to that belief. The kahunas say that all convictions about reality are either accepted or established by the conscious mind, and are therefore potentially available to it for examination at any given moment. This is essentially

the same as Freud's finding that "the pathogenic idea
. . . is always lying ready 'close at hand,' "[11] except that
Freud was referring to memories and the kahunas refer
to beliefs, of which memories are only representations.
The kahuna idea is also contrary to the psychoanalytical
model which implies that memories and beliefs which
cause present effects are hidden from the conscious
mind.

When beliefs about reality are accepted by the
conscious mind (*lono*) as unalterable facts, then for all
practical purposes the mind cannot "see" them as beliefs,
and may therefore feel helpless in the face of their
effects. A person who accepts the "fact" that he has an
incurable disease may succumb to his belief, even though
many others have successfully cured themselves of the
same illness. Much of kahuna healing is involved with
helping the *lono* of an individual to change its view of
apparent facts. Feelings and emotions are considered by
the kahunas to be energetic responses to the stimulation
of belief patterns, and as such are meant to inform the
conscious mind of what beliefs are in operation. Ideally,
the *lono* can then choose to follow emotions through, not
to respond to them, or to redirect them. But without an
understanding of their nature, a *lono* is likely to treat the
feelings and emotions themselves as facts over which it
has no control. Again, this is not a novel concept. Freud
recognized that ideas could stimulate feelings which
could be converted through suppression into physical
symptoms, and this is the underlying basis for modern
psychosomatic medicine. Maltz says that an emotion is
"in the nature of a sign or symptom," that it is "like a
thermometer which does not cause the heat in the room
but measures it."[12]

In addition to the faculties of awareness, analysis,

integration and volition, the kahunas attribute to the conscious mind the important faculty of creative imagination (*laulele*), whereby you purposefully imagine a condition that you strongly desire to experience as a physical reality. It is by the use of this faculty that you can consciously develop new skills, expand your awareness, solve problems, change beliefs and direct energy. The kahunas lay great stress on the training of this faculty because of its tremendous importance in directing the activities of the subconscious (*ku*) and in providing patterns for the Higher Self. Carl Jung was one of the first Western psychologists to emphasize the use of creative imagination, and it is growing more and more popular as people become aware of its potential.

The Subconscious (*Ku*)

The *ku* self, or "body mind" as it may be called, is somewhat analogous to the subconscious in Western psychology, but a better analogy might be a living, nonmaterial computer. Maltz uses this analogy, too, though he tends to equate the subconscious with the brain. The kahunas would be more likely to say that the brain is the physical expression or tool of the *ku*, but this distinction does not appear to have any serious practical consequences. Kahunas will use whatever analogy suits their purpose and aids understanding. In old Hawaii the *ku* was compared to a servant. A modern kahuna working in an industrialized society is more apt to use the computer analogy.

Essentially, the functions of the *ku* are to maintain the integrity of the body and oversee its operation, to receive perceptions and transmit them to the conscious mind, to store memory, to generate, store, distribute and transmit energy, and to follow orders. In fact, all the functions of this part of the mind could be condensed into that last phrase. Above all, like a good servant or a computer, it follows orders. The *ku* responds to two types of "programming": instinct and habit. Instinct, as defined here, refers to all the so-called involuntary functions of the body such as growth, development, maintenance, and sensory or "extrasensory" reception or transmission. The kahuna idea is that these are programmed into the *ku* by the god-self (*aumakua*) at the time of conception. From this viewpoint, the DNA molecule would be an expression of such programming and not a cause. Habit includes all behavior programmed into the *ku* directly or indirectly by the conscious mind (*lono*). It is learned behavior, as opposed to instinctive. Direct programming would involve the applied will of the *lono*, as in learning to drive a car; indirect programming would involve allowed learning, such as the acceptance and incorporation of a parent's fear of snakes or the so-called hereditary predisposition toward a certain kind of disease. None of the above appears to be at serious odds with the new psychologies; Maltz and Assagioli give very similar descriptions of this aspect of the mind.

The urge toward the formation and maintenance of habits is a major characteristic of the *ku*. Without this urge you could not survive, because you would not be able to learn and retain the techniques of survival. However, habits may either inhibit or encourage growth and development of mind and body, depending on their nature. This fact forms the basis for behavior modification techniques, although the kahunas would not agree with the behaviorist view that thoughts can be explained in terms of implicit muscle behavior. Instead, they take the view that all habits are mental, and that physical responses are the result. Even Maltz, in describing happiness as a mental habit, is really talking about emotional habits. For the kahunas, the distinction between mental, emotional and physical habits is an important one, but this does not seem to be the case in modern Western psychology.

To continue with the computer analogy, in kahuna terms it can be said that a program corresponds to a belief or a set of beliefs, and that a habit is the running of the program, or the carrying out of a belief. All habits are based on one or more beliefs. By a cooperative process between the conscious mind and the subconscious, various beliefs and habits are organized into a gestalt which becomes the individual's personality. As mentioned, the *lono* aspect has the capability of examining these beliefs and of changing them, thereby enlisting the cooperation of the *ku* and the *aumakua* (Higher Self) in changing habits, personality and circumstance.

The Body (*Kino*)

The physical body, *kino*, is conceived of by the kahunas as an intensely energized thoughtform. This is evident in the roots of the word itself:

ki—to emit, a bundle (of thoughts), force	*kia*—to concentrate thought
	ino—very much, intensely
ki'i—image	*no'o*—thought

The body is held to be an idea of the Higher Self expressed into physical form, modified by the beliefs of the conscious mind and maintained by the body-mind or subconscious. It is an expression of the self, as a painting or a sculpture is the expression of an artist. The body is both a means of projecting ideas into the physical world and an ideal feedback device for experiencing the effects of those ideas. Your state of health, physical development, moods and feelings are all expressions of ideas, and subject to alteration by a change in your conscious thinking. The concept of the body as a thoughtform is quite esoteric, compared with modern psychological thinking. The latter tends to treat the body as a purely material entity subject to the effects of thought, but certainly not as being an effect of thought. Assagioli, who comes close to kahuna thinking in many ways, considers the body in mechanical terms. He teaches that the patient must dis-identify with the body and emphasizes that "it is only an instrument." His purpose is to enable the patient or subject to become aware of himself as a center of consciousness and to be free from interpreting experience only in terms of physical sensations and behavior. WK's opinion is that, while such a procedure might have temporarily bene-ficial effects, it engenders a false sense of separation which could inhibit the achievement of mastery over bodily functions and lessen one's sense of responsibility for the body's behavior. As he puts it, "Of course you should not identify yourself only with your body; you are much more than your body. But it is your creation and that is why it responds to your thoughts."

Related to the body is the concept of the etheric body (*aka*). Here we range very far from modern psychology's center and right to its outer fringes. Briefly, the *aka* body is something like an invisible, duplicate body taking up the same space as the physical one, and providing the essential pattern around which the physical body is formed. The *kino aka* may be considered as the basic thoughtform of the Higher Self (*aumakua*), a kind of blueprint. The natural tendency of the body-mind (*ku*) is to follow this pattern, but it must also try to follow the pattern from the conscious mind (*lono*), as represented by learned beliefs. Distortion, that is, illness, results when the ideas of the *lono* are different and intense enough to conflict with the basic pattern. The kahunas feel that it is because of the existence of this basic etheric pattern that healing of the body can take place, for without such an overall pattern there would be nothing to guide the *ku* in making repairs. I have been unable to find anything as plausible in modern psychological or medical literature relating to the means by which the body knows how to return to a state of health.

Biological Energy Flow

The kahunas say that the means by which mind affects matter is *mana*, the life force. In terms of the physical body, this energy manifests itself both as a flow or current, and as a field. A rough analogy is that of an electric current and its surrounding magnetic field. The known electrical properties of the body are considered by the kahunas as by-products of the *mana* current and field. The main source of this energy is the Higher Self, which provides it in a way that is inexplicable in strictly physical terms. The best analogy I can come up with is that of a "white hole" in the center of your being through which energy comes streaming from another universe. There is also an interaction with fields and currents in the environment, primarily through what are commonly called *chakras* in yoga philosophy or acupuncture points by Chinese healers. The principle points of interaction or interchange are those located along a line running from the perineum up the front and back of the body to the fontanel, as well as others on the hands and feet. In addition, life force or *mana* is absorbed from the environment through breathing and eating. Techniques for increasing your supply of *mana* beyond the normal (accumulating a "surcharge" as Long puts it) are similar to other approaches found around the world, namely specialized breathing and exercises, the eating of special foods and drinks, visualization, the use of natural or man-made "*mana* generators" such as crystals and pyramids, and the stimulation of the interchange points. Also used is the conscious generation of emotion.

Western psychology and medicine seem to be taking an increasing interest in the above concept, and increased research is going on now. However, this interest is not really new. Josef Breuer, a colleague of Freud, wrote at length about "tonic excitation," the transmission of psychical energy through the nervous system in a way comparable to electricity flowing through a wire. It was Wilhelm Reich, though, another colleague of Freud, who carried the concept of psychical energy into the domain of a physical, measurable force. His extensive researches into "orgone energy," as he called this force, resulted in healing devices (banned for human use by the FDA) and also led to what today is called "bioenergetic therapy." Reich definitely recognized the link between bioenergy (*mana*) and disease. As he said of one patient:

> Her fear of moving her neck existed long before the collapse of the vertebra. Indeed, her manner of holding her head and neck was only part of a general biophysical attitude which we had to understand not as the result but as the cause of her cancer.[13]

Apparently, however, Reich never got to the point of seeing beliefs as the cause of emotions, or at least not directly. Reich listed twelve properties of orgone energy which would also apply to *mana* as bioenergy. Five of the most important are listed below:

1. It would be fundamentally different from electro-

magnetic energy and yet related to it.

2. It would have to exist in non-living nature independent of living organisms.

5. It would permeate and govern the *entire* organism instead of being limited to individual nerve cells or groups of cells.

7. It would manifest itself in the production of heat.

10. It would be capable of *charging* living matter; thus, it would have a *life-positive* effect.[14]

Having built and experimented with a large number of orgone energy devices, and having worked for many years with various forms of *mana*, I can state my definite opinion that the two are identical.

Maltz also speaks of a non-specific life force as being "the secret of healing,"[15] but apart from a few people who are following up Reich's work, most of the present research into *mana*-type energy is being done by parapsychologists working with so-called psychic healers. Dr. Thelma Moss, a medical psychologist at UCLA who has done extensive research with these healers through the use of Kirlian photography, feels that "there is an 'energy flow' from the healer which initiates and augments the patient's self-repair system."[16] Nevertheless, the concept of a life force manifesting as a current and field seems to be outside the mainstream of psychosomatic medical practice in the West.

Emotions

The kahunas consider emotion as the sensation of the movement or excitement of energy in the body while accompanied by a particular thought, and the roots of all Hawaiian words that refer to emotions contain this idea .

of movement. It is quite common in Western psychology to discuss emotions in terms of energy flow, whether thought of as an actual energy or not, but to the kahunas it is important to realize that an emotion is not just a movement of energy. Energy movement can be felt without emotion. Just stand up, run in place very fast for a few seconds, stand still, and you will be able to feel a tingling movement of energy through your body that has nothing to do with emotion as we usually define it. For the kahuna, what distinguishes emotion is the associated thought, for it is the thought that makes it an emotion. In working with many people I have discovered that they find it difficult, if not impossible, to tell the difference between anxiety and anticipation or anger and enthusiasm, once the associated thoughts and images have been cleared away. In most of the Western psychological literature I have studied, the writers speak of different emotions and their effects, but they tend to equate emotions with thoughts or else they tend to separate emotions from thoughts.

According to the kahuna teaching, an emotion arises when a belief or belief complex is stimulated by an external or internal event, such as a thought or memory. This causes the discharge of a current of energy through the body which acts as a carrier for the content of the belief, much as electricity going through a telephone wire can carry the content of a conversation. The conscious mind (*lono*) perceives this as an emotional feeling, while at the same time the subconscious (*ku*) puts into motion a programmed or habitual reaction to the belief, unless directed otherwise by the conscious mind (*lono*). An example would be remembering an insult, getting angry again, clenching your fist automatically and getting a headache. Part of kahuna training is concerned with helping the conscious mind learn how to perceive emotions without allowing the subconscious to engage in habitual action. What may seem like emotional control in a well-trained kahuna is actually a conscious directive not to follow through with a habit pattern, achieved by using muscular relaxation to separate thought from action (as will be described). The training also consists of learning to "read" the information content of the emotion in order to discover the belief which is its source, if this is not immediately apparent. Once it is known, the kahuna can introduce a new belief to cancel out the old one and create a better habit to replace the less effective one.

The intent of the kahuna determines what happens to the energy discharge of the emotion itself. He may redirect it in any number of ways, but the most common technique is to relax and allow it to dissipate. Since all emotions induce muscular tension as a preparation for action—most easily noticed in the well-known "fight or flight" response—the conscious relaxation of the muscles has the effect of switching off the habit reaction, thus dissociating the energy from the thought that stimulated it. You can experience this for yourself by relaxing your muscles as much as possible and then trying to get angry, using memory or any other means. You will find that, as long as your muscles remain relaxed, it is physiologically impossible to get angry. This free energy is then automatically dispersed through the body and into the surrounding field. If the kahuna wants to use the energy for another purpose, such as healing, he will relax the muscles and then go through a process, perhaps visualization, to channel the energy into another response pattern. This is very much like the relaxation and imagery techniques proposed by Dr. William Kroger with the help of hypnosis. Other techniques the kahuna might use are simple attention and volition, controlled breathing, and what might be called "nonjudgmental focus." The latter is a form of concentrated, nonanalytical awareness or meditation that is quite refreshing and physically beneficial.

The Nature and Formation of Complexes

There has been some discussion of beliefs and belief complexes, but now I want to cover them in greater detail to show more fully the kahuna view of how they affect the life of an individual.

A belief can be defined as any idea that you accept as true—an idea that either validates or does not invalidate personal experience. The kahunas treat beliefs as more or less enduring patterns of thought which are literally *incorporated*, i.e., taken into the body, and which govern or influence all mental and physical behavior. With the exception of the behaviorists, nearly all modern psychologies admit the importance of beliefs as factors that influence health and disease. Kroger emphasizes the necessity for changing both attitudes and behavior, and Maltz says of the self-image that:

> Once an idea or belief about ourselves goes into this picture it becomes "true" as far as we personally are concerned. We do not question its validity, but proceed to act upon it *just as if it were true.*[17]

For the most part, however, the word *belief* is used to cover all sorts of ideas, thoughts, opinions, attitudes, etc., without any attempts to differentiate beliefs in terms of the intensity and effects they have. The kahunas make precise distinctions which they feel are vital to the process of treatment for positive change. Dr. Oyle comes close to the kahuna view when he says: "An idea which carries an emotional charge of energy is called an *opinion*. A rigidly crystallized opinion carries a higher emotional charge and is called a *belief*."[18] The kahunas go even further and break down beliefs into three categories: assumptions (*paulele*), attitudes (*kuana*), and opinions (*mana'o*). These English translations are only approximations used for the sake of discussion. It might be easier to understand the differences if we use the analogy of water. Assumptions can be considered as beliefs which have become crystallized in consciousness, like blocks of ice. They deal with generalities about life and self and are not easily changed. Attitudes are liquid beliefs. They are more easily changed, but change may involve emotional conflict. Opinions are gaseous, like water vapor, easily changed with little emotion. The latter kinds of beliefs have relatively little effect on habitual behavior by itself, so the following discussions will be concerned with the first two categories and the resulting belief complexes.

Assumptions (*Paulele*)

Paulele has the meaning of "confidence" and "to stop jumping around," implying a state or condition of security. The assumptions people hold about themselves and about life in general are considered by the kahunas to be the foundation on which people base all their behavior. The assumptions provide a framework through which experience is measured, tested and evaluated, and which determines the response to experience. As such, they provide a sense of security, even when experience is negative. Assumptions are absolutely necessary in order to be able to function in this world, and most of them are learned early in life from parents, relatives, peers and authority figures. A child has to make assumptions about life in order to survive, and one of the first assumptions made is that the parents must know what life is all about and therefore their assumptions must be valid. Actually, children will rarely accept all the assumptions held by parents and others, but instead will pick and choose by some inner decision process that no one else can fully know. In a given family, one child might accept a parental belief that the world is a dangerous place. Another child in the same family might reject that and decide that the world is a friendly place, yet accept his parents' belief that some kinds of people are inferior. The assumptions that are accepted become the programs that determine behavior, both mental and physical, and they also act as blueprints for the Higher Self to form experience.

Assumptions enter through the conscious mind (*lono*), the interpreter of experience, though usually at a level which might be called "semi-conscious." The kahunas do not have a concept equivalent to Freud's "unconscious," because for them there is no such thing as nonawareness, merely differing degrees of awareness or states of attention and nonattention.

If an assumption about reality is not consciously rejected, or if it does not directly conflict with existing assumptions, then it is accepted as truth by the individual. Once incorporated, assumptions are generally forgotten, even though they continue to operate. This does not mean they are lost to conscious awareness, but only that the *lono* mind no longer pays any attention to them. It is something like forgetting about your underwear during the course of a day, although it's always possible for you to remember it. In the case of assumptions, they become such a familiar way of interpreting the world that they are completely taken for granted. The kahunas do not accept the idea that the root causes of behavior are buried in the past or in some part of the mind accessible only to a trained expert. All beliefs are available consciously at any moment, but you won't be aware of them if you've forgotten them or don't want to look at them for some reason. The conscious mind is like a dark room full of furniture, and conscious awareness is like a flashlight that can reveal only a limited number of items (beliefs, memories, thoughts) at one time, but which has the potential for shining on anything in the room. If you get used to looking in one direction, you may forget about the antique on the shelf behind you; you may take the wallpaper for granted and not look at it any more; and you may have a drawer full of scary stuff that you never want to look at again if you can help it. Sometimes an expert can help you remember what you have forgotten or help give you the courage to look at what frightens you, but he can't do anything that you aren't capable of doing for yourself.

In a sense, the subconscious mind (*ku*) is in charge of incorporating assumptions into your memory and behavioral system. There is no volition involved here, merely the urge to follow orders like a computer. An assumption acts like a prime directive and the *ku* can only obey to the best of its ability. Assagioli proposed the following psychological law with which the kahunas would disagree:

> All the functions, and their manifold combinations in complexes and subpersonalities, adopt means of achieving their aims without our awareness, and independently of, and even against, our conscious will.[19]

The idea of a battle of wills between the conscious and

subconscious minds is considered an invalid concept by kahuna teaching. The only battle is between the present will of the conscious mind and the ongoing effects of what it has willed in the past.

Attitudes (*Kuana*)

If assumptions are likened to a foundation, then attitudes are the structure built on that foundation. Attitudes may also be called "coping beliefs," because they develop as a means of coping with aspects of experience that are not neatly covered by the assumption. They are more specific than assumptions, and they cover the grey areas of experience where some belief is necessary in order to act, but the belief is still open to doubt. Because attitudes are less secure than assumptions, people will often defend them with more emotion. When they are questioned, a person is forced to face his own insecurities, and this often gives him the sensation of being attacked to the point of requiring an emotional defense. Such resistance to threatening ideas has long been noted by Western psychologists. Freud said:

> It has indeed been generally admitted by psychologists that the acceptance of a new idea (acceptance in the sense of believing or of recognizing as real) is dependent on the nature and trend of the ideas already united in the ego.[20]

He went on to say that an idea not compatible with existing ones would provoke "a repelling force of which the purpose was defense against this incompatible idea." As you know, some of the most emotional responses occur when questions about race, sex, religion and politics are raised, which says something about the security of the attitudes involved.

When assumptions are questioned, however, the

reaction is usually one of surprise that something so obvious should be questioned at all. Maltz described such a case in this way: "Tell the schoolboy that he only 'thinks' he cannot master algebra, and he will doubt your sanity."[21] Since there is seldom strong emotional reaction when an assumption is questioned, some kahuna healers identify attitudes and assumptions by the reaction to challenging them, and modify treatment accordingly.

Attitudes derive logically from the underlying assumptions, because the *ku* is profoundly logical. Those who feel that the subconscious is unreasonable and illogical will always be in a quandary as to how to deal with it, but once you realize that it is as logical as a computer you will have the key to creating change. Now once the subconscious has incorporated an assumption, it will create logical attitudes based on it in order to cope with direct experience, but it will always present these to the conscious mind in some fashion for approval before turning them into habitual behavior. Depending on how your mind works, you may deliberate for a long time before accepting the attitude, or you may accept it in the wink of an eye and promptly forget about it until it gives you trouble.

Attitudes are logically derived, but not everyone uses the same kind of logic. Below are some kahuna views of how different attitudes might arise from the same basic assumption. In both cases a dependent assumption is also noted. This is an assumption that you accept as true about life, but which is dependent for its existence on the acceptance of the basic assumption.

Subject 1. Basic Assumption: This is a hostile world. Dependent Assumption: The best protection is flight. Derivative Attitudes: If this is a hostile world and the best protection is flight, then (a) my best protection from hostility is to avoid it; (b) I must let others have their way so I will not get hurt; (c) I must hide my talents and abilities or I will be open to attack; (d) I must pretend to be weak or extra nice so as not to invite attack.

Subject 2. Basic Assumption: This is a hostile world. Dependent Assumption: The best defense is a good offense. Derivative Attitudes: If this is a hostile world and the best defense is a good offense, then (a) my best protection against hostility is to counterattack immediately; (b) I must be strong enough to defend myself; (c) I must never show weakness; (d) I must be suspicious of the motives of others; (e) I must get what I can before others take it away.

Of course, the above examples are simplified for the purposes of illustration. Nevertheless, it can be seen how the varied attitudes of two such subjects could result in quite different personalities, even though they share the same basic assumption about life. Their attitudes would also govern their reactions to sickness, relationships, goals and every aspect of life. And their assumptions, say the kahunas, would ensure that they would encounter a great deal of hostility. If you take the "self image" as a set of assumptions, Maltz seems to be speaking for the kahunas when he says:

> The self-image is a "premise," a base, or a foundation upon which your entire personality, your behavior, and even your circumstances are built. Because of this our experiences seem to verify, and thereby strengthen our self images, and a vicious or a beneficent cycle, as the case may be, is set up.[22]

Complexes (*Hilina'i*)

A belief complex is a system of associated ideas composed of one or more assumptions and the attitudes that are attached to them. The kahuna term for a belief complex, *hilina'i*, can be translated as "a braid for trying to understand something." In Huna symbology, complexes are represented by braids, nets, spider webs and bramble thickets. The first two are used for complexes in general, while the last two are usually reserved for restrictive complexes.

In practice, people have numerous complexes which are necessary in order to cope with life. This is like saying that you have to have beliefs in order to experience and deal with anything, and what you experience and deal with depends on the nature of your beliefs. A complex, in kahuna terms, may be either positive or negative, and the only way you can tell that is by the effects on your life. Since a complex consists of all your beliefs about any particular subject that are consistent with each other, there is real trouble when you have two complexes on the same subject that are in conflict.

Maxwell Maltz drew much of his inspiration for *Psycho-Cybernetics* from Prescott Lecky, a psychologist who taught that the personality is a system of ideas (beliefs) that must appear consistent with each other to the person holding them. Ideas inconsistent with this system are rejected, not believed, and not acted upon. From the kahuna standpoint, this is oversimplified. They see the personality as a system of systems, a grouping of complexes, some of which may or may not be consistent with each other because they are based on different assumptions accepted from different authority figures at different times. For example, the two subjects described in the previous section shared the same basic assumption but had different dependent assumptions, and these gave rise to different attitudes. Now, it would be possible for one person to have accepted one of those dependent assumptions from his mother and a different one from his father. The result might be two separate complexes in serious conflict, with resulting personality distortions and a great deal of unhappiness. An idea that is inconsistent with *all* a person's complexes will be rejected, as Lecky proposed, but an idea inconsistent with some complexes may be accepted by others. In extreme cases this may produce a "split personality," but more commonly it simply produces different reactions under different circumstances. An example of this would be a man who has a "different" personality when at work, at home or at play. Each of these situations would trigger different associations and reactions from various complexes within his total personality.

Unfortunately, it seems that many people have varying numbers of conflicting assumptions and attitudes woven together into restrictive or negative complexes. *Negative* here refers to belief complexes that are ineffective, that do not satisfactorily resolve life's problems from the individual's point of view, and that are in conflict with other beliefs. One term for such a complex is *kuku*, which means "brambles, thorns, crowded, to be in competition." The duplication of the word *ku*, the aspect of mind that is in charge of holding beliefs, gives the connotation of a subconscious that is overworked.

The kahunas teach that belief complexes act as guidance systems for the flow of the life force, *mana*. Where there is conflict, the flow is distorted, and this distortion may lead to acute or chronic tension on a muscular, organ or cellular level. Such tension can lead to pain and illness, and this is the basis for the kahuna teaching that the source of all illness can be found in conflicting ideas. The generic term for illness in Hawaiian is *ma'i*, meaning "a state of tension or restriction," in other words, stress. Some doctors and psychologists define stress as environmental conditions that require behavioral adjustment, but for the kahunas this is putting the cart before the horse. They see stress as an internal reaction to environmental conditions (including thoughts as part of the personal environment), for it seems apparent to them that similar conditions do not cause similar reactions in all people.

Ecological Feedback

In kahuna teaching, belief complexes do not merely affect thoughts, emotions, reactions and the physical body; they also affect the way you perceive the environment and even determine what your environment is. One way to look at this is to realize that you perceive according to your beliefs, and whatever does not conform to your beliefs is ignored. However, the kahunas add an esoteric dimension to this by saying that your beliefs are the channels through which your Higher Self literally produces experience. Thus, a complete individual—*aumakua, lono* and *ku* combined—forms his own experience, which he then perceives and reacts to. The practical kahuna application of this concept comes under the heading of what I have termed *ecological feedback*.

Feedback is a process in which the result modifies the factors producing the result. It's like playing tennis and watching where the ball hits so you can adjust your grip to make a better hit next time. Ecology is the interrelationship of organisms to their environment. Ecological feedback as I use it describes the process by which you become more aware of your environment (including your physical body as well as your surroundings) in order to find out what kinds of beliefs led to the formation of that environment. The equivalent Huna term is *unuhi ao*, "to interpret the waking world." Once the beliefs at the root of experience are consciously recognized, they can be changed if desired, and thus cause the environment to change. This concept, far different from that held by most modern psychologists, is one with far-reaching implications.

By studying your illnesses, for instance, you can discover first the attitudes and then the assumptions that produced the types of illnesses you tend to have. At first glance this does not seem to be very different from a technique used by Freud of working backwards through chronologically associated memories to reach what he called the "pathogenic nucleus." But the difference is profound because Freud worked with the memories of events and not with the beliefs about the events. When you work with uncovering beliefs, memories may pop up in any order or not at all.

Most modern psychologists and physicians define certain illnesses as psychosomatic (caused by mind or emotions) and others as strictly organic (caused by outside agents or hereditary factors). Howard R. and Martha E. Lewis, authors of a book called *Psychosomatics*, wrote that "Researchers are finding that people with certain character traits are likely to suffer from certain illnesses." Then they state:

> Excluded from most discussions of psychosomatics, however, are such strictly inherited conditions as hemophilia and sickle-cell anemia. Also not considered in the realm of psychosomatics are diseases caused by environmental factors such as food poisonings, occupational diseases, and poisoning from

pollutants. On the other hand, it is possible that in such cases the level of impairment may be caused by psychic stress.[23]

The kahunas would say that not only the level of impairment, but the attraction of the condition itself is caused by psychic stress. They recognize inherited predisposition to certain illnesses, but more in terms of inherited beliefs in cellular memory, rather than physical inheritance. As for such conditions as flu epidemics, WK has called them primarily "media-genic," meaning that they are caused more by the media than anything else. His explanation for why the infamous "swine flu" never reached epidemic proportions is that people didn't like the name and didn't believe in it because they thought it was politically inspired. In the Huna teaching all experienced events, including illness and accident, originate in the mind.

Since so many beliefs are reflected in the physical body, kahunas specializing in this area pay more attention to *where* a disease manifests than to what kind it is. Modern psychosomatics appears to go along with this to a considerable extent, and Reich noted that in his day most cancers occurred in the genital and erogenous areas of the body. The general kahuna teaching as I learned it says that conflicts in competence and communication manifest in the head, shoulders, arms and hands; conflicts of affections, responsibility and self-worth manifest in the area between the solar plexus and the neck; conflicts of security and authority occur between the solar plexus and the upper thighs; and conflicts regarding support and progress manifest in the legs and feet. Using this framework, the body, like the rest of the environment, can be "read" to reveal source beliefs. Ecological feedback includes paying attention to recurring thoughts and daydreams, the content of spontaneous speech patterns, and recurring emotions, all of which are means of tracing out beliefs. Such factors are also used in modern psychosomatic treatment, but the emphasis there is more on changing behavior than changing beliefs. The kahunas would say that changing behavior is merely one way of reinforcing belief changes, and that behavioral change itself is dependent on changes in thinking.

Beliefs are the basis of all experience, say the kahunas. Reality is not objective but subjective. Kristin Zambucka, mentioned previously, writes: "An attitude is ours to control. We are the creators. Change your thoughts and you change your world."[24] Curiously, this kahuna idea of reality as totally subjective has its counterpart in modern particle physics. Fritjof Capra, a physicist who has compared modern physics with ancient East Asian philosophy, speaks of a theory of today's physics in this way:

> The basic structures of the physical world are determined ultimately by the way in which we look at this world . . . (and this) reflects the impossibility of separating the scientific observer from the observed phenomena . . . in its most extreme form it implies ultimately that the structures and phenomena we observe in nature are nothing but creations of our measuring and categorizing mind.[25]

Yet, as will be seen in the next chapter, the kahunas are capable of working with belief in objectivity in order to effect a healing.

 CHAPTER 5

Healing Methods

Kahuna healing involves the whole person—the Higher Self, the conscious mind, the subconscious and the body—and the person's environment. Since its purpose is to bring about a healing and not to prove a particular method, it is geared to individual needs. The same kahuna might use quite different methods to treat two people with identical symptoms because their beliefs might be quite different. And beliefs, according to Huna, are at the root of all illness.

The kahuna idea of working with beliefs to initiate healing is reflected in the general Hawaiian term for health and healing, *ola*. This little word, which has many more meanings all related to improving one's whole life, is perhaps best translated as *enlightenment* (*o*—to enter; *la*—light, a symbol for understanding and power). Specific symptoms are treated as part of the overall healing process because it is recognized that they merely serve to mask the true cause of illness. The Hawaiian word for symptom is *ouli* (*ou*—to hide; *li*—emotions such as fear and anger). Somehow the kahunas recognized very early what modern psychosomatics calls the conversion reaction and what Freud called hysteria, or the conversion of an emotional condition like anger into a physical symptom like a migraine headache. The difference is that the kahunas considered all symptoms as some form of conversion reaction, even to the point of including personal circumstances such as accident proneness, poverty or loneliness.

To say that working with beliefs is at the foundation of all successful therapy is almost equivalent to saying what hypnosis is, defining that term very broadly to include the idea of accepting suggestion at all levels. As Jay Haley, in his book *Uncommon Therapy*, says, "The influence of hypnosis upon all forms of therapy has not been fully appreciated. It can be argued that most therapeutic approaches have their origins in that art."[26] In a sense, it could be said that all kahuna healing methods are based on hypnotic suggestion—understood as the changing of beliefs—and that all non-hypnotic methods used by them are merely intended to facilitate this process.

"Strategic Therapy"

The approach whereby the therapist initiates treatment based on particular patient needs has been called "strategic therapy" by Haley in writing about the psychiatric techniques of Dr. Milton Erickson, author of numerous articles on hypnotherapy and one of the most outstanding practitioners of that art. "Therapy can be called strategic," Haley says, "if the clinician initiates what happens during therapy and designs a particular approach for each problem."[27] It is not known for how long kahunas have been using this approach, but WK claims that it has been for centuries. Speaking for the West, Haley says it has only begun to proliferate since the middle of this century.

Kahuna strategic healing methods can be roughly classified under the headings of the Material Approach, the Energy Approach, and the Mental Approach. The way in which they are applied and combined depends on the nature of the illness and the belief system of the patient. Kahunas will always work within the patient's belief system, because to do otherwise would invite resistance to the healing process. A person who believes firmly in medical treatment will be treated accordingly before or along with methods that will get closer to the cause, as modern psychiatrists often do. A person who firmly believes in curses will be treated on that level first, though Western practitioners are not likely to go that far. Still, the awareness of the value of such an approach by some modern therapists is made clear in a statement by Kroger: "We are well aware that faith in a specific cure leads to the success of that cure!"[28]

The Material Approach

This includes the use of medicine, diet, ritual, amulets and anything else which involves the introduction of an object or formal event into the healing process. There are two logical bases for this approach. One is the fact that, for the most part, people are brought up to believe that matter or outer events are more real than thought. The kahunas turn this belief into a tool to help the healing. The second basis is the fact that certain medicines, foods and energized objects actually do interact with the body's metabolism.

Much more so than the other approaches, this one is highly dependent on the acceptance of the authority of the healer by the patient. WK says that modern medicine is primarily faith healing. The reason doctors have as much success as they do regardless of what kind of treatment they give is because their skill and knowledge are trusted by so many. This is why placebos can be so effective. If the patient believes strongly enough in the authority and skill of the healer, he can heal himself even without "real" medicine.

Medicine.

The kahunas have a distinctly unorthodox view of the effects of medicine, based on their idea that illness is not caused by bacteria, viruses or carcinogenic agents, but by tension resulting from conflicts of thought and emotional energy. Epidemics, according to this view, are caused by individual reactions to social telepathy, and not by spread of infection from exterior factors. Although Reich did not mention telepathy as a factor in disease, he did hold the opinion that the effects of infection originated within the individual as a result of acute or chronic tension. After examining some of the inconsistencies of the theories of infection current in his time, Reich said, "If this question is thought over carefully, the scientific worthlessness of the air-germ theory will have to be admitted."[29] Let me emphasize that the kahunas do not claim that germs or microbes do not exist, but only that they are catalysts or by-products of disease and not its cause. If there were no fear or undue tension in people, there would be no disease, regardless of the presence of bacteria or viruses associated with illness.

A word is in order here about the epidemics of smallpox, measles and venereal disease that nearly wiped out the Hawaiian population shortly after the coming of the

Europeans and Americans. According to the kahuna view, this was a result of infection by ideas more than by microbes. At this time the dominant kahunas had lost most of their healing knowledge, the *Lono* doctors and herbalists were few and far between, the religious and legal structure of the Hawaiians was in disarray, and the foreigners came with incredible displays of material power and knowledge accompanied by equally strong beliefs about guilt and sin. Small wonder that so many Hawaiians succumbed and so few kahunas could help.

The kahuna belief that illness results from tension is borne out in the roots of the Huna term for medicine and medical treatment, *la'au lapa'au*. This term clearly indicates the kahuna stand that the function of medicine is to stimulate an excitement of energy flow in the body which will aid in breaking up the tension-induced illness. For this reason, the kahunas define medicine more broadly than in the West. In addition to chemicals and herbs, they include parts of fish, animals and plants whose names, nature or appearance signify healing characteristics. Colored lights, clothing and objects are used, too, for their psychological and physiological effects. Squid would be used because its Hawaiian name (*he'e*) has the connotation of illness fleeing away; pork might be used because of a similar connotation in a Hawaiian word that resembles the word for pig; sugar cane (*ko-kea*) might be used because the name means "to succeed in making something clear"; and a red object could be used because the color red, a sacred color, was associated with blood and divine power or *mana*. In addition to these psychological effects on the subconscious, the kahunas appreciated the physical effects of certain ingredients, but only for their energy-stimulating or muscle-relaxing effect, not their ability to "attack" anything supposedly invading the body. The latter is the product of a society with fearful beliefs about reality.

WK has mentioned a form of Hawaiian kahuna medicine that I believe is worth more investigation. Probably the best translation for it would be "aromatherapy." This term has been used in the West but primarily refers to the use of flower essences to be applied as ointments or taken internally, as in the "Bach Remedies" developed by Edward Bach, M.D. The kahuna use involves inhaling fragrances directly and assumes that the essence of the material being inhaled will go straight to the bloodstream via the lungs and act more quickly than something swallowed or placed on the skin. Although incense and perfume are used in the West and East to create moods and influence emotions to a certain extent, I have not found much in the way of a direct medicinal use of aroma comparable to the kahuna idea except for the use of inhalants to relieve respiratory congestion. However, I did come across a comment by a French essayist Michel Eyquem de Montaigne who wrote in the sixteenth century:

> Physicians might (in my opinion) draw more use and good from odours than they do. For myself have often perceived, that according unto their strength and qualitie, *they change and alter, and move my spirit, and worke strange effects in me.*[30]

Another commonly used form of "medicine" favored by kahunas is plain water, infused by the kahuna's *mana* and accompanying thoughtforms. Typically, a kahuna does this by focusing *mana* out of his hands or breath into the water while concentrating on a healing image. Naturally this is most effective when the patient is told what the water will do for him, but the effect is greater when the water is "charged" than when it is not, regardless of whether the patient witnesses the charging. This is definitely outside the realm of Western orthodoxy, which would probably claim that the water would act more as a placebo than anything else. Nevertheless, Charles Panati, a writer on parapsychology, tells of experiments performed by biochemist Justa Smith with a healer which seem to show conclusively that a type of energy transmitted from the healer's hands actually modified enzyme solutions. This same healer was tested under very strict conditions by Dr. Bernard Graf at McGill University in Canada. The healer merely held bottles of water between his hands for a period each day. Plants watered from these bottles grew significantly better than control groups. An easy way to charge water for taste as well as health is to leave a bottle of it in direct sunlight for an hour or more, like people do for "sun tea." I have experience of this working, though I had no control group for corroboration. I used water charged like this in a green bottle for two German shepherds who were going to be put away because they couldn't keep food down. In two weeks they were happy and healthy.

Diet.

Diet is given importance by the kahunas because it is felt that the kinds of foods you eat habitually reflect your state of mind. Changing your diet, therefore, helps to change your state of mind. Once I was about to have a meal with friends when one asked me, "What do kahunas eat?" With a smile I answered, "Anything they want to." I mention this because kahunas as a group do not follow or recommend for general use any special kind of diet. Some are vegetarians and some are meat-eaters, and I suspect that some don't eat much of anything at all. As one great kahuna said, "It is not what goes into a man's mouth that defiles him, but what comes out of it." However, kahunas are likely to recommend plenty of "living" or fresh, raw fruits and vegetables because these are thought to contain more *mana*. As a matter of fact, the root meanings of the Hawaiian word for food, *'ai*, link it directly to *mana*, and the roots of the word *kahuna* include the idea of his being a cook, one who prepares and shares power with others. In a book by June Gutmanis about kahuna herbal doctors, it is noted that the kahuna therapist prepared the healing meal.

The lack of vitamins and minerals in a person's body is not thought to be caused by an inadequate diet, but by certain types of thinking that result in an imbalance in the body's metabolism. The use of supplements helps to restore the body's equilibrium temporarily, which at least gives the person an opportunity to straighten out his thinking. The kahunas teach that the healthier your mind is, the more you will be able to self-generate all your needed vitamins and minerals, no matter what your diet.

In the Western medical tradition, diet is used as a major tool for controlling weight, but with the kahunas diet would play a very small role in such treatment. The kahuna would be much more concerned with the person's attitude about himself and his weight, and whether or not the weight interfered with his effectiveness in living. There is nothing wrong with being "overweight" or "underweight" in the kahuna view, since those terms are only meaningful in relation to some arbitrary social standard. A fat person can be just as healthy, happy and effective as a slim one. It is not the weight itself that matters so much as the possible use of the weight for self-punishment, avoidance of relationships, as a substitution for affection, a withholding of emotional expression, etc. In general, the kahuna view is that the state of being overweight or underweight according to social measures is not something to be treated unless it is also a symptom of inner conflict. And then it is the thinking and behavior that must receive the most attention. Once that is taken care of, the body will adjust itself.

Fasting was not part of the Hawaiian healing tradition, but it has been used by kahunas elsewhere. WK has the following comments to make on it: Ordinarily, the body operates on the energy supplied by the food and air you take in daily. In fasting, the body must begin to operate on its energy reserves. These are usually thought of in terms of stored fat and protein, but energy is also stored in the form of chronic muscular tension. During fasting, this tension energy is called upon for body operation as well. Since the tension areas are intimately connected to belief conflicts, they will surface as the energy is utilized and the tension is relieved. This is often accompanied by a cathartic emotional release and the dramatic elimination of symptoms of illness. Fasting, when it is used as a tool, is not done for "purification" of the body, but as a means of exposing and draining the energy from deep-seated complexes. Even then, it is only a step in the treatment process, for without a change in thinking the benefits of fasting will be temporary.

In my studies of related literature, only Reich had anything specific to say about cathartic emotional releases due to the release of chronic muscular tension, but for his patients this was brought about by massage and/or the use of orgone field energy. As far as I know, the kahuna view of the effects of fasting is unique.

Ritual.

Ritual plays an important role in most healing practices, whether by kahunas or modern doctors. It includes everything in the healing situation which has no direct effect on the healing, but which serves to convince the patient that the right thing is being done by the right person. Thus, a ritual in this sense would include anything from an ancient kahuna dancing and chanting while rubbing the patient with *ti* leaves, to a white-jacketed modern doctor sitting in an office filled with success symbols and calmly telling the patient that he knows exactly what to do. Ritual helps to establish confidence in authority, and this helps to open the patient's mind to the healing process. Other forms of ritual used in the West are formal hypnosis, meditation and group therapy sessions. Of course, ritual may also be engaged in by the healer in order to convince his own subconscious that he has the power to heal.

Charged objects.

Objects that the kahunas consider to be strong sources of *mana* are frequently used because the introduction of more *mana* into the body from whatever source often acts to relieve tension and therefore symptoms as well. The kahunas feel that they can personally charge an object with their own *mana* for this purpose, and Long describes this at length along with reports of experiments to demonstrate its validity. On the beach at Waikiki near the Surfrider Hotel, there are four "healing stones" that local legend says were filled with *mana* by departing Tahitian kahunas centuries ago. However, the kahunas also make use of natural sources of *mana* such as stones and crystals, certain woods, and special sites where *mana* is supposed to be more abundant. In *Nana I*

118

Ke Kumu Mary K. Pukui, a Hawaiian lady with a rich knowledge of Hawaiian lore, says that "In Hawaiian belief, *mana* could be emitted from a rock, the bones of the dead, the medicine that cures or the potion that kills."[31] One of the favorite healing woods was ebony, called *lama* in Hawaiian. The Pukui-Elbert *Hawaiian Dictionary* has this to say about it: "*Lama* wood was used in medicine and placed in hula altars because its name suggested enlightenment; huts were built of *lama* wood in a single day during daylight (*lama*) hours, and the sick were placed inside them for curing."[32]

It is impossible, of course, to completely separate the direct effect of medicine, diet, and charged objects from the patient's reaction to the setting or ritual and the authority of the healer, but the kahunas are not interested in such distinctions so long as there is a beneficial effect. This is a point of radical difference between the kahuna and most Western approaches to healing. Western orthodox practitioners are likely to discard or prohibit any treatment method which does not fit within a relatively narrow range of acceptability. For instance, this Skinnerian view still prevails among orthodox psychiatrists and physicians: "Since mental or psychic events are asserted to lack the dimension of physical sciences, we have an additional reason for rejecting them." And Oyle, a medical doctor, says, "Most of my colleagues believe to this date that in the space where the body organs are supposed to be, there is only matter."[33] Naturally, such a view drastically limits the kinds of treatment that will be accepted and allowed. This makes sense when a particular form of treatment represents an actual danger to the patient, but many methods so banned do not fit that category. It would seem that they are banned because they are not part of the accepted tradition, and any successful applications are discounted. And this occurs in spite of the fact that many accepted methods have dangerous side effects. Oyle reports that the Food and Drug Administration "announced that fifteen people had been killed by Clindamycin and Lincomycin 'which are often prescribed by doctors for the treatment of acne and the common cold.' " He also reports that his successful nondrug and nonsurgery clinic was closed simply because it was too unorthodox. The Western establishment appears to emphasize method rather than results, and unorthodox methods are usually rigorously shunned and sometimes emotionally attacked. Reich, whose books were banned *and burned* by the U.S. Government in the 1950's, called this attitude "emotional plague." By contrast, the kahunas will use any method that works, as long as its side effects are not serious. Their emphasis is on results and they know that methods are always secondary to beliefs.

The Energy Approach

This approach takes three forms that can be called physical, current, and field manipulation, although this verges on hairsplitting since a kahuna may use the three forms simultaneously. All have the purposes of releasing energy that is blocked by tension, stimulating the flow of bioenergy to promote self-healing, and reinforcing healing suggestions given by the healer.

Physical manipulation.

There are three subdivisions of this form of energy stimulation: *lomi, lua* and *hula.*

1. *Lomi* is a direct massage technique applied to muscles that are in a state of acute or chronic tension. It

is usually done by hand like Swedish massage, but in old Hawaii a specially carved stick was used for deeper massage. A variation is *'a'e*, referring to a way of massaging the back with the feet.

2. *Lua* is a form of hand-to-hand combat like karate, also practiced for sport, exercise and as a means of discharging emotional tension. One root translation of the word is "to cast off grief completely."

3. *Hula* is generally thought of in the West as nothing more than a graceful form of Polynesian dancing, but the modern entertainment is based on an ancient system for body enlightenment and spiritual development. A root meaning of the word is "to raise the sacred flame," a reference to an energy flow like that in kundalini yoga. Even in its present form the leg, hip and upper body movements are conducive to the release of muscular tension blocks. A similar effect is achieved by the ancient Chinese *T'ai Ch'i Ch'uan* and modern aerobic dancing, though in very different ways.

Current manipulation.

There are two main forms of current manipulation used by the kahunas, both based on the idea that *mana* flows like a current in the body.

1. *Kaomi* is a technique similar to acupressure and consists of applying a downward pressure at special points on the body. The stick used in *lomi* is sometimes used in *kaomi*, too, but it is more common to use the fingers or the heel of the hand. In cases of blockage, the patient may feel a sharp pain like a needle prick when the pressure is applied. Anyone who has experienced reflexology, a kind of foot massage, will know what I mean. Sometimes symptom relief is immediate and sometimes several such treatments are required, depending on how

chronic the condition has been and how fearful of change the patient is. The concept is that the pressure stimulates an increased interaction between the point of pressure and the *mana* in the environment or in the healer's hands, which results in an increased flow that acts to break up tension.

2. *Kahi* is a technique of applying gentle pressure to tension areas or of lightly stroking the area with the open hand. To an observer, the first way might look like the "laying-on-of-hands" practiced by some Western evangelists and modern nurse-healers who use "therapeutic touch," while the second might look more like caressing. The secret to the effectiveness of this technique in relieving symptoms is the amount of *mana* emitted by healer's hands. This technique can be used by anyone because everyone emits *mana*, but the more *mana* emitted, the more effective it is. To increase the emission, a kahuna might use visualization, a brisk rubbing of his palms, or especially a positive emotion like love. It is no accident that a variant word, *kahiau*, means "to give generously or lavishly with the heart and not with expectation of return."

Field Manipulation.

This method, sometimes called *manamana*, resembles *kahi* in appearance, except that the hands of the healer do not touch the patient. Instead, they are generally held a few inches to a foot away from the skin or clothing. The healer builds up a surplus of *mana* in himself through various techniques already described and transfers this to the field of the patient by means of his hands, his will and his imagination. The idea here is that a kind of induction effect takes place in which the flow from the healer charges the patient's field, inducing a current flow in the patient's body.

An unusual variation sometimes used is to discharge the patient's field, which also seems to induce a current flow. Broadly speaking, charging is most useful in cases of fatigue, depression and injury, while discharging is most useful where hypertension, anxiety and swelling are present. The subjective effects of charging or discharging may vary considerably, even when the patient is not aware of what the healer is doing. In field manipulation, the patient frequently reports sensations of warmth, tingling and/or interior movement or release. Nearly always, the kahuna will use verbal or telepathic suggestion to aid the process. Because this is such a nonmaterial treatment method, it is far outside the orthodox Western system. However, therapeutic touch, a modern technique very similar to this kahuna method, is being increasingly accepted in hospitals where nurses use it in addition to orthodox therapy. It is taught in the graduate school of a major university which is a leader in the training of nurses, and workshops in it are held in hospitals nationwide and in other countries. I have also heard a number of doctors mention privately that either they or someone they knew had and used this ability but they were afraid to let their patients know about it. Even Wilhelm Reich, who was hardly orthodox, never wrote about this method, but in a personal conversation a former colleague of his said that he was present on one occasion when Reich apparently used such a method to heal a baby.

I would like to end this section with just a word on the supposed effects of this kind of healing on the healer. I have met quite a few "psychic healers" who report feeling completely exhausted after giving a number of healings using their hands. From my kahuna studies I have learned that this is because they are trying to use their own personal energy and are not building up a surplus beforehand or, even better, allowing energy to flow through them rather than from them. Also, they may be subconsciously resisting the process or the great patient-load or whatever, causing muscular tension which will result in fatigue. Anyone who heals in the kahuna way will end up feeling even better than when he started. Another supposed adverse effect is the healer's "picking up" the patient's illness through the energy field. I have seen (and used) many simple and elaborate ways to avoid this. I have learned, though, that the illness is not in the energy field but in the thoughts of the patient, and a healer can pick up the illness only by being open to such thoughts. Some healers perform little rituals such as flicking their fingers to wash away or discharge the patient's energy. The only purpose this serves is to convince the healer's subconscious that he is safe. There's nothing wrong with that, but if you thoroughly believe that you won't be affected, then you won't be, with or without the ritual.

The Mental Approach

This method has to do with teaching the patient how to use his own mind more effectively, but with no attempt at mind control by the healer. It is by far the most important method in the healing repertoire of the kahuna and is considered as the core of all healing, since all experience is a reflection of thought.

For the purpose of discussion, the outline of this approach is presented as steps in a process, but it should be understood that in actual practice the application of the steps is not as distinct as given here. The process for teaching a person how to take charge of his own thinking and healing is based on a four-step training process that the kahuna himself undergoes.

Awareness of Thoughts (*Ike*).

If you are going to consciously change attitudes and assumptions, you must first be aware of the ones you have. It may sound obvious, but most people pay too little conscious attention to what they think and say in terms of the potential effects of these on their lives. Therefore, in the beginning of treatment, a kahuna may help the patient become aware of habitual speech patterns, inner dialogue and imagery themes. Attention to recurrent feelings, dreams and external conditions may also be encouraged. By giving his attention to these factors, the patient becomes aware of how he has been reinforcing his undesirable circumstances.

A patient who is used to suppressing undesirable thoughts may need considerable assistance in bringing them to conscious attention, as many psychologists and psychiatrists have discovered. One technique the kahunas use to aid this process is guided imagery, the stimulation of *makaku* imagination. *Makaku* translates as "originating in the *ku*" and refers to spontaneous or stimulated imagination that reveals patterns of beliefs. As I have mentioned previously, this is becoming more and more popular in the West.

Occasionally, as sometimes happens in psychoanalysis, the mere awareness of undesirable habits of thought or speech will be enough to cause the patient to make immediate changes in thinking, with resultant benefits to the body or circumstances. But all too often awareness doesn't produce any change at all. The kahunas teach that this is because all ongoing experience is maintained by habits, and awareness alone doesn't change a habit. The only way to change a habit is to replace it with another habit, which leads to the next step.

Establishing Goals (*Makia*).

The goals meant here include developing new beliefs and habits and also the laying out of plans for the future. The patient is helped in developing a clear idea as to what kind of health, personality and environment he wants to have, and he is aided in understanding what will have to be done to achieve what he wants. A major technique used in *makia* is *pa laulele*, which I call "see and be," and which involves strongly imagining a desirable circumstance and putting yourself into the picture with all your senses. It is something like the state of mind of a mime during a performance. What this does is to "pretrain" the subconscious and the body and prepare them for the new experience. For instance, in the case of an ongoing chronic condition—physical, personality or environmental—you would first establish the new goals/beliefs/habits that would apply, and then use your imagination to preexperience the new condition. Some Western psychologists, too, prescribe this technique. Kroger calls it "sensory imagery conditioning," and Maltz describes a virtually identical technique. Assagioli justifies this approach by stating a psychological law that "images and mental pictures tend to produce the physical conditions and the external acts corresponding to them."[34]

Short, emotionally charged self-suggestions or affirmations are also used with *makia*, but it is important that the patient be well trained in how to do this effectively so that the suggestions actually help to bring about the new condition and don't merely result in suppressing what he doesn't want to be aware of. To be effective, a suggestion or affirmation has to be believable to some degree. Saying "I am healthy" when one is sick, or "I am happy" when one is sad, may work for some people but not for others. The use of strong emotion helps here, as do techniques like hypnosis that quiet the critical-analytical part of the conscious mind. If there seems to be a significant subconscious resistance to change, then the kahuna will go on to the next step.

Changing (*Kala*).

This word has outer meanings of release, freedom and forgiveness, but the roots give the meaning of changing one's path. To forgive, for instance, is to change the way you have been thinking about someone or something. For *kala* to be effective, you have to be consciously willing to make the change and to give up old ways. Without some positive motivation to change on the part of the patient, even if received telepathically, the kahuna will not usually even attempt a healing. Kroger would agree. In regard to chronic alcoholics, he says that one "who does not wish to be helped, or who is literally brought in . . . against his will, cannot be helped by any psychotherapeutic approach."[35]

Once the patient is aware of inner conflict in regard to changing a habit, a common technique is to immediately replace the negative thought, feeling or action with its opposite. Since chronic muscular tension is brought about by a distortion of energy flow sustained by particular habits of thought, according to Huna theory, a release of tension will occur when the undesirable thoughts are replaced by beneficial ones. Freud sometimes achieved this effect by "erasing" negative memories and substituting positive ones. The key factor here for the kahunas, though, is replacement, not suppression

127

followed by substitution. For some people this is not so easy because the habits they have may serve an unknown purpose. So when the kahuna feels it is appropriate he may explore the patient's memory with him in order to reinterpret or even modify past events. The kahuna may also teach techniques of muscular relaxation, for when the muscles are relaxed it is physically impossible for negative emotions to arise and for unwanted actions to take place. Negative thoughts may still occur, but with the muscles relaxed the habitual reaction to them is switched off and the subconscious (*ku*) is more receptive to the installation of a new habit pattern. This is precisely what happens in hypnotherapy.

The main tool used to alter negative thinking is volitional imagination, or *laulele*. As you may recall, this is imagination in which the content is consciously chosen by the individual. It would be more accurate to say the vital content, because nearly all imagination includes at least some spontaneous elements (*makaku*). The deliberate imagination (*laulele*) acts like a pattern to channel the thoughts, emotions and actions into new directions. Once this imaginative pattern is established as a new habit, it becomes *makaku* or spontaneous. However, this involves the next step.

Directing energy (*Manawa*).

This word has meanings of channeling and directing *mana* continuously and persistently. It involves the actual establishment and maintenance of new habits of thought and behavior, which can only be done by practice and more practice. *Manawa* includes, too, the use of anything which will reinforce the new habits you are trying to establish, such as books, lectures, symbolic pictures and objects, rituals, physical surroundings, association with people who have the desired qualities, etc. More than anything, though, it involves action and emotion, which means the participation of the subconscious (*ku*). The kahuna reasoning is that ideas do not become materially effective unless they become part of the *ku* mind. Knowledge which remains intellectual is no more than opinion, and as such has little effect on the world or the individual. That is why another word in Huna for enlightenment is *na'auao*, which can best be translated as "gut knowledge."

Treatment Failure

In spite of skilled treatment and the best of intentions, many attempted healings either fail or are temporary. Although the kahunas realize that poorly applied treatment can be a factor, they would not quite agree with Kroger's assertion that "If a therapeutic procedure fails to produce a change in the patient, the fault lies in the experimental technic, and not in the patient."[36] Fault is not the issue at all, and to a very large degree the success of therapy does rely on the skill, knowledge and flexibility of the healers. But for the kahunas the single reason underlying all others in treatment failure is that there has not been a change in thought habits on the part of the patient. This is seen not as a fault but as a fact. Better methods might help or they might not, but nothing will happen regardless of method unless the patient's thinking changes. The kahunas give several reasons why the patient may not be willing to make this change.

The first reason might be called "cost-benefit resistance." This occurs when the patient claims to have a desire to be cured but is receiving psychological, emotional or physical benefits from the existing condition that outweigh, in the patient's mind, the benefits to be derived from the cure. In other words, the cost of the cure will include giving up the present benefits of the condition, and the patient is not willing, either consciously or semi-consciously, to make that sacrifice. Present benefits might include sympathy, attention, revenge, desire for control, financial security (as with a patient receiving disability payments), emotional security (as with a patient who will have to face undesirable responsibilities if cured), suffering (as with a patient who believes he deserves to be punished), and the security of familiarity with his present state. When this kind of resistance is encountered, no relief or very temporary relief will be obtained, no matter what treatment method is used. It would be up to the healer or therapist to convince the patient that there would be greater benefits in changing than in persisting in the present state, though in some cases it is the patient's subconscious (*ku*) that has to be convinced.

The next reason is lack of confidence in the healer or in the treatment method being used. Open-minded skepticism is not usually a problem as long as the healer has confidence in himself and in what he is doing. But fear and distrust on the part of the patient, if maintained, will result in temporary effects at best. The skill of the therapist or healer is of course an important factor in this kind of treatment failure, but the kahunas insist it is not the determining factor as the source of the patient's fear and distrust may have nothing to do with the therapist's skill.

The most prevalent reason for treatment failure is lack of attention to the attitudinal aspects of the condition. When symptoms alone are treated and there is no corresponding change in the patient's attitudes, relief is always temporary. What confuses Western doctors, say the kahunas, is that a patient may express the same negative beliefs through different symptoms. The doctors treat the symptoms as different entities while the underlying cause is the same. So-called "faith healers" run into a similar problem. True faith healing is a healing of beliefs, and if that takes place the cure is permanent. Most of what is done under that name, however, is nothing more than energy manipulation. When the energy is sufficiently intense, as in a charismatic revival meeting, spectacular results can be achieved. But hours, days or weeks later, if the thinking of the person involved has not changed permanently, the energy will dissipate and the old symptom will return. Also under this category of lack of attention to causative attitudes is the failure to take into account the patient's home or work environment, particularly the people in it. Since symptoms are expressions of attitudes, some symptoms are the results of attitudes about other people, and in their presence the symptoms may be aggravated. This is why a person can be "cured" in a hospital only to fall ill again when sent back home. Whenever possible, the kahunas will include family and friends and enemies in the treatment, even if only in imagination.

Finally, when the individual's Higher Self has made the decision for the physical self to die, there is nothing that can be done except perhaps for symptom relief. However, no one else can know if this decision has been made irrevocably, so the kahunas feel it is quite proper to continue treatment as long as the patient is willing and able to receive it. They do not believe in the idea of "karmic interference." Some healers worry that they might be interfering with a person's karma, or preordained fate, by attempting a healing, and they tend to think this may be operating whenever they encounter difficulty in a healing. The kahunas consider difficulty as a challenge. Their word for fate is *hopena*, which means "the result of what has gone before." To them, that means you create your own reality. If you are a healer and there is a person in your life who needs healing, then you are a part of that person's fate and he is a part of yours. Since fate is not preordained, according to the kahunas, you cannot interfere with it in the sense of obstructing it, but you can change it as long as all parties involved agree at some level to the change.

Divine Healing

So far the most important element in kahuna healing has not been mentioned. This is the god-self, *aumakua*, or, in simple terms, God. All healing, in the kahuna view, is really nothing more than the result of a natural communion with the god-self, or allowing its source energy to flow freely along the original pattern in the etheric body (*aka*). Illness and distortion of any kind result from interference with that flow. The most direct healing of body, mind and circumstance comes through consciously involving the god-self in your daily life and thoughts in an open, loving and trusting way. The practice of love (*aloha*) which includes the experience of sharing joy, is the way to make this union materially effective. Joy is life-giving and expansive, and when it is made part of your life it automatically releases tension and acts like an invitation to the Higher Self to become a full partner in bringing forth health, happiness and fulfillment. As taught by the kahunas, joyful cooperation with "god-in-everything" is the best medicine for all ills, the best solution to all problems, the best way to achieve personal fulfillment. To do this, however, takes a commitment to remind yourself constantly of the presence of God in all people, places, things and situations. This practice has brought me personally more joy, happiness, health and success than anything I have ever done. How do you go about it? Well, I have experimented with many methods and the best one for me came from a science fiction book by Robert Heinlein entitled *Stranger In A Strange Land* (which, by the way, happens to contain an ancient kahuna ritual of water-sharing). In it is a simple phrase used by the hero: "Thou art God." Say it in your mind to all and everything, including yourself, from the time you get up till you go to sleep; *believe it* and your life will be renewed.

In Closing (*Panina*)

Some people have asked how I can justify revealing the kahuna knowledge like this. They are familiar with other groups who guard their secrets like precious gems that might be defiled if someone else looks at them, or out of fear that others will find they have no gems. I need no justification because we have no secrets. Huna is the secret that is meant to be revealed; the kahunas are its guardians and not its jailers. I share the cry of the oracles of Old Hawaii that sounded out from the temple grounds:

Let that which is unknown become known!

Epilogue

Following is the account of an experience I had that now now seems almost like it happened to someone else. I wrote this account shortly after it happened, and looking back from the perspective of quite a few intervening years I'm almost embarrassed by the fervor and improbability of it, and by the fact that I've not lived up to the task assigned me. But it did happen, and I'm still trying, and the name *Kaula* now evokes a kind of "future self" who helps me to help others. This was a mystical experience in physical surroundings, the kind that cannot help but change a person's life.

"On Labor Day weekend of 1975 I was camping with my family and several friends at a campground called Happy Gulch at the foot of Mt. Able in the Los Padres National Forest. During the evening of August 30 we had all enjoyed the brilliance of the stars and the great number of meteors that flashed through the sky. However, the cold soon forced us to retreat to the comfort of sleeping bags.

Epilogue

"In the fullness of night I was awakened by a voice from within. Checking my watch I saw that it was nearly 2:00 a.m. The voice was urging me to get dressed and go outside, which I found myself doing without hesitation. The night was clear and warmer than it had been when we went to bed. The stars seemed even brighter and there was still no moon. The air was undulating with that peculiar wave motion which indicates an intense field of mana, and I was aware of a deep humming sound that seemed to vibrate through everything. It was nothing mechanical, but rather a living pulsation. The inner voice urged me to hike up the road to Mt. Able, which I did, passing the sleeping figures of my companions. Later I learned that they, too, had heard the humming, felt the power in the air, and had been called by an inner voice. But being unfamiliar with the area they thought it more prudent to remain in camp.

"I walked for a long time, aware only of the humming and the mana, until my inner voice told me to stop and sit on a point overlooking the valley to the west. As I sat I looked up at the stars and they were moving in large, irregular circles all over the sky. I blinked my eyes and shook my head, thinking it was an optical illusion, but no matter how I tried to look they kept moving. Then suddenly the humming increased, a tingling went all through my body, and a scintillating rainbow appeared before me, hanging in mid-air beyond the edge of the cliff. In the same moment I began to hear the murmuring of millions upon millions of voices from all around me and even inside me, from the stars, the air, the plants, the earth, from cells, molecules and atoms. Gradually I was able to perceive that all these myriad sounds were speaking as One, in unison. And they were speaking to me, calling me by my initiatory name.

" 'Kaula, Kaula, know that I AM, always, everywhere, everything. I AM the Nameless One of many names, the Soundless One of many voices. Kaula, be my prophet, my warrior of Light, my emissary, my Child of the Rainbow. Gather my children and help them experience My Presence. Teach Love, Kaula, for Love is the key to all. Love is the Path, Love is the Secret. Teach Love, Kaula, and Love Me.'

"Unable to speak, I sent out a feeling of love to the whole universe and was instantly flooded with a return flow so great that I entered a timeless, spaceless state of pure bliss in which all conscious thought disappeared. I was myself, and yet I was All. I was a blade of grass, vibrating with tremendous inner strength as I slowly and inexorably pushed aside a rock thousands of times heavier and harder than myself. I was the rock, locked in a strange crystalline life cycle attuned to galactic time. I was a bird, warm and cosy under my ruffled feathers, asleep and dreaming my own unsharable dreams. And a tree, a coyote, an ant, a house, a comet, a cloud, the universe entire one at a time and all at once. And I was I.

"At some unknown point I was brought back to here-and-now bodily awareness, still trembling from the ecstasy. The rainbow was gone and the voices were stilled, but sitting around me were all the teachers who have helped me in this life. My earthly father was there, wearing the costume of the Silver Circle. There was Wana Kahili, who initiated me as a kahuna, M'Bala, the feticheur from West Africa, Sufi Joe the Persian, Gordo the brujo, Fa Hsien the Chinese lama, Ra Ptah, Manea, Lucius, Rufus, Jarod, Naran, and others. They were all as real as the ground I was sitting on, and I would have loved to greet them each with a hug, but I sensed that the occasion was too solemn for that. Nevertheless, I felt the

136

warm greeting of their thoughts. After a few moments a sharp feeling of expectation became apparent. Then Wana Kahili and my father, who were sitting directly in front of me, moved apart and a white-robed figure with a cowl suddenly appeared between them. There was a period of intense silence and then the figure threw back his cowl and revealed a face of such beauty that I could scarcely keep my eyes on it, yet I was compelled to do so. At every instant his face changed shape, nationality and sex, retaining its inner glow throughout the process. As his face changed I received an inner picture of association. He was an artist of Mu, an Atlantean scientist, a Lumanian explorer. He was Gautama the Buddha, Moses on the Mount, Jesus of Nazareth and Mohammed the Prophet. He was Pele, Kuan Yin and Mary, Viracocha, Quetzacoatl and Kanaloa. He was the manifested Christ, the Enlightened One, the Teacher of Light.

"A certain time passed and then he and all my teachers spoke with one voice, telepathically, directly into my mind. First, they reminded me of the plan formed ages of Earth-time ago and in which I had agreed to play a role along with hundreds of others. Next they reviewed my present life from infancy onward, including my errors and wanderings from the path, as well as my initiations and successes. They pointed out my remaining weaknesses and neglected strengths and advised me on corrective measures in order that I should be able to fulfill my mission.

"Finally they confirmed what I had read on the tablets in Hawaii and explained the connection with my mission. When this was over, the Christ stood up and walked toward me, stretching his hands out over my head. I immediately felt his power flowing into me and filling me with Light as he spoke these words:

" 'Kaula, be thou anointed with the power of the Holy Spirit as one of my priests and prophets of the New Age. Go forth and teach and write of the presence of God, of the meaning and way of Love, of the vast power and potential of the human mind. Go forth and heal the sick in mind, body and heart, and teach them also to heal themselves and others. Counsel, instruct and open the minds of all who come to you, using that knowledge of mind, matter and energy which has been given you, and prophesy as you are guided by the inner light. Establish temples of wisdom throughout the land where this knowledge may be taught and practiced, and establish also communities where love and freedom prevail. Gather around you fervent disciples to train and ordain to do all these things as well. Use the means of the world to gain these ends. You will always be guided by the inner light. Yours is the way of Huna, the science of Love, the path of Harmony on and with the Earth, the universal knowledge. You and those whom you guide shall call yourselves Children of the Rainbow, as was done of old. The rainbow, the star of seven points and the cross of life shall be the symbols of your way.

" 'Innumerable are the paths to God, so be at peace with the paths of others, for they, even unknowingly, are following Huna when their path is true. As a last word, begin to prepare your people for the time of Great Emigration, for assuredly mankind has already chosen as its destiny a return to the stars.

" 'Now we take our leave, though we remain in touch through Spirit. Tell no one of what you have seen or heard until you receive a sign. Then you shall make this experience known, begin to write down the knowledge of the tablets and commence the great work. And always remember, Love is the key.'

Epilogue

"With this the face of the Christ grew brighter and stabilized into the smiling features of a great being from a far, far distant place whom I have seen in previous visions. Then he touched the top of my head with his finger and I passed into unconsciousness. When I awoke I was alone in the stillness. And the new dawn broke as I made my way back to camp."

The Kahuna Code

It seems to be a fairly frequent occurrence among some humans to want to hide what they are saying from others, and the most common way to do this throughout history has been to use some kind of secret code for communication. This obviously has practical advantages in politics, war and in times of religious persecution. Leonardo da Vinci taught himself to write upside down and backwards so that no one could read his notes unless they knew the trick of using a mirror. Sometimes a rare language is used instead. It is not unusual for priesthoods to have a special ancient language used only by initiates, and during World War II the United States successfully used Navajo communicators to confound its enemies. Childhood mock languages such as pig Latin and Hong Kong serve the same purpose. And in ancient Hawaii, the chiefs had artificially constructed secret languages known generically as *kake* so they could talk around commoners without being understood.

However, that which is called the "kahuna code" does

not fall into the same category. The purpose of the code was not to keep things secret but to keep the knowledge available. I have theorized elsewhere that Polynesian was artificially constructed on somewhat the same manner as Esperanto, only with more success. In any case, the kahunas transmitted their knowledge through the root meanings of their language, using special rules to extend those meanings. By this technique, a great amount of information could be transmitted by a single word when properly broken down. As long as the language remained in existence, the knowledge would continue to be available to anyone who understood the technique. Of course, if the technique were forgotten, then the coded information would be lost even though the language remained. This is what seems to have happened to a large extent in Hawaii after the thirteenth century arrival of Paao. In fact, one translation of that priest's name is "a limitation of knowledge."

WK and Long both feel that the kahuna code is most easily interpreted from the Hawaiian dialect of Polynesian, so that is the basis for code references throughout this book. The source used for root meanings is the *Hawaiian Dictionary* by Pukui and Elbert, with elaborations provided by WK and my knowledge of Hawaiian culture.

Hawaiian is a rather simple and highly flexible language based on relatively few sounds. As transliterated into English, there are only seven consonants, H, K, L, M, N, P and W (sometimes pronounced as V), and five vowels of A, E, I, O and U, which makes twelve letters. There is also a glottal stop (') which replaces a hard sound used elsewhere in Polynesia and which can therefore be considered as a letter, too. However, in modern Hawaiian, especially as used by non-Hawaiians, the latter

141

is often omitted. Among some Hawaiians with strong Tahitian ancestry the letter K is in certain cases replaced with T. Thus Westerners have become familiar with the *ti* plant and *tiki* dolls, although in the original Hawaiian they would be pronounced *ki* and *ki'i*, respectively. It should be noted that Melville disagrees with this, and claims that T was used in the original Hawaiian and that, for some mysterious reason, the missionaries forced the Hawaiians to use K.

Since linguistic nuances are unimportant to this book, it can be said that for all practical purposes the consonants are pronounced as in English, and the vowels as follows:

a as in f*a*ther   *o* as in m*o*te
e as in toup*ee*   *u* as in l*u*te
i as in mach*i*ne

The glottal stop is like the sound between the syllables of the exclamation "oh-oh" in English.

Rules of the Code

According to WK, the rules below are used for uncovering the information encoded in a word, using the word *kahuna* as an example.

1. First the meanings of the word as a whole are examined.

2. Then, where possible, the whole word is broken into separate words, such as *ka huna* and *kahu na*.

3. Next one looks for words within the word, as *kahu, ahu, huna,* and *una.*

4. The individual syllables are also examined: *ka, hu* and *na.*

Appendix

5. The vowels are doubled as well: *ka'a, hu'u,* and *na'a.*

6. And the syllables are doubled: *kaka, huhu,* and *nana.*

7. Further extensions of meaning can be found by adding various vowels to the individual syllables, as in *kai, hui* and *nai.*

8. Even more extensions are uncovered by treating the word as an anagram, which would give combinations such as *haka, aka, hana* and *kanu.*

9. Finally, a proper decoding requires a knowledge of poetic, legendary, figurative and symbolic references, as well as a sense of context.

Decoding the information in a key Hawaiian word may therefore be considered an art as well as a science. Nevertheless, most of the meanings can be ascertained by anyone with access to a good Hawaiian dictionary.

Examples

Since the word *kahuna* was used to demonstrate the rules of decoding, let us examine it according to those rules in order to discover what the kahunas thought about their own profession.

Kahuna means "priest, minister, sorcerer, expert in any profession; to act as a priest or expert."

Ka is a root word with many meanings, though it is usually translated as the article "the." It can also mean "of, or belonging to." Other meanings are "to hit, strike, thrust; to bail water; to clean (as weeds or mud from a pond); to make nets and to knit; to turn the soil or turn a rope (as in jump rope); to remove (as a cataract from the eye); to snare (as birds); to curse; to send out a vine or to send forth shoots; incoming (of a current); to cause something to happen." As applied in the word *kahuna*, the meaning of hitting and thrusting refers to the forceful use of energy or *mana*. Bailing water refers to a kahuna's ability to reduce or draw off another person's life force (*mana*). This is an effect of the death prayer, but it can also be used in a healing way to calm down a highly emotional individual. Cleaning out weeds has to do with removing attitudinal barriers to a free flow of the life force, since one of the symbols for that force is water. A net is a symbol for a psychological complex or set of beliefs, not necessarily negative. To make a net or to knit, then, refers to a kahuna technique for constructing a new set of beliefs. To turn the soil refers to the kahuna's role as an agent of change. To remove (as a cataract) again has to do with removing psychological obstructions. A bird is often used to symbolize an idea or a person. To snare refers to capturing ideas or strongly influencing another person. The reference to cursing is meant to show that the kahuna powers can be used for good or evil. Sending out a vine is a symbolic reference to telepathy. An incoming current (as of water) refers to the kahuna technique of increasing one's available supply of life force. Causing something to happen is a direct reference to a kahuna's ability to manipulate circumstances.

Huna means "minute particle, small, little; hidden, secret, to conceal or disguise." *Huna* is the generic term for the knowledge of the kahunas. *Ka-huna*, therefore, can be translated as "the secret," or more accurately as "that which is hidden, concealed or not obvious." The meaning of "minute particle" reveals that *huna* is something hard to see or recognize, not necessarily concealed on purpose. There are other words with that meaning.

Kahu means "master, honored attendant, guardian, nurse, keeper, administrator, pastor; to tend or cook at an oven; a cook or to cook; to burn (as lime in a pit); to seethe with hot rage." This word demonstrates the role of a kahuna as a master and guardian of hidden knowledge (*kahu-huna*) and also one who cares for others. The idea of seething with rage and burning inconspicuously (as lime) refers to a kahuna's use of intensified emotional energy (*mana*) for healing and other work, as fire is another symbol for *mana*. The concept of a kahuna as a cook will be dealt with in the next paragraph.

Ahu means "a heap, pile or collection; an altar or shrine; an oven; a short cape or cloak." Now, this is where some extended knowledge is necessary in order to understand the full import of this word and the previous reference to cooking. In connection with cooking in an oven there is an implied reference to food, particularly plant food, since meat was cooked in a pit. The word for plant food is *'ai*, with additional meanings of "to eat; and to exercise and enjoy the privileges and responsibilities of power or rule." To the Hawaiian mind, the cook (*kahu*) who uses fire (*mana*) in an oven (*ahu*) to prepare (*kahu*) food (*'ai*) is a direct representation of the guardian or master (*kahu*) who uses the life force (*mana*) at an altar (*ahu*) to pile up or collect (*ahu*) power or authority (*'ai*)—in other words, a kahuna. The short cape or cloak worn by chiefs and kahunas of old Hawaii was a symbol of their authority and power.

Una means "to send or transmit, to command, to put to work; to send spirits on an errand; fatigued, weary; to pry (as with a lever); to urge, disturb, harass." Here the reference is to the kahuna practice of telepathic influence, healing, or even harm. Fatigue or weariness, i.e., a loss of life force, was a symptom of the action of the death prayer.

Hu as a word means "to rise or swell (as yeast); to ferment, overflow, percolate, effervesce, boil over; to surge or rise to the surface (as emotion); to roar, grunt, hum; a spinning top; to depart from the proper course, to miss the way; to unite or join." The references to overflowing and surging have to do with conscious use of emotional energy to carry out certain kahuna practices. Roaring, grunting and humming refer to the use of sound in generating such energy, and a spinning top symbolizes the energy in motion. Departing from the proper course shows again that the energy can be misused. The idea of joining in this context refers to the use of the energy to make contact with the objective of a particular practice, and also to a kind of psychological integration.

Na means "calmed, quieted, pacified, assuaged, soothed, settled or resolved; and to moan, groan or wail." This is a reference to the kahuna ability to heal and resolve problems. The moaning, etc., refers to the role of sound in relieving stress and achieving a state of calmness.

Kaka repeats some of the meanings of *ka*, such as hitting and thrusting, and has the additional connotation of "to fish with a net." Fish and water were symbols for memories in the subconscious (*i'a* is fish; memory is *hali'a*, which means essentially "to carry a fish.") Fishing with a net, therefore, refers to a kahuna practice somewhat similar to psychoanalysis.

Huhu means "to cherish; rotten; angry, offended; to scold or become angry." In Hawaiian, the doubling of a

146

syllable is often used to show intensification. In this case, the reference is to intense emotion, which can be either positive or negative.

Nana means "to plait, weave or knit; still, calm; to prophesy; to come to life or activity, to show liveliness, animated, stirring of life; to spread; snarling, to strut, sexually excited, aggressive; to look at, observe, pay attention to, take care of; to soothe or quiet." The knitting, etc., repeats a meaning of *ka*, and the references to stillness and calmness relate back to *na*. It often happens that code words include opposite meanings, which serves to demonstrate the kahuna philosophy of the relativity of life, similar to the yin/yang concept of the Chinese. So in this case we have a word meaning calmness that also means activity and aggression. Aggression is to be taken in a positive sense of movement or communication. Probably *assertiveness* would be a better word. Paying attention and observing are meanings relating to the necessity for a kahuna to achieve a high state of awareness in order to carry out such practices as prophecy.

Ka'a means "to roll, twist, braid, turn, revolve; to reach or be in a state of; to take effect; gone, absent, past, turned over, transferred, delivered; to pay, paid; to manage, be in charge of; well-versed, skilled; tale, legend; thread, line." Here is some repeating of the meanings of *ka* with interesting extensions. The reference is again to the kahuna's role as an agent of change, helping people to overcome the effects of the past and to learn to manage and take charge of their own lives, which takes skill. Tales and legends refer to information contained in past events as well as the kahuna use of teaching stories, and thread refers to the link between past and present and the use of telepathy.

Hu'u is not used as a word in Hawaiian.

Na'a duplicates the meanings of *na*.

Kai has several of the same meanings as *ka* and also means "to lead, direct, or do something deliberately; to train (as for a race)." The reference is clear, especially the idea of the need for practice and conscious application. *Kae* has opposite meanings having to do with negative and positive emotions and actions. *Kao* has meanings of striking and thrusting, as well as references to the need for self-discipline and the dangers of using too much power. *Kau* is a word with many meanings, the most important of which have to do with the ability to accomplish things within a context of time and the use of reason. It also duplicates meanings of several previous roots.

Hua means "fruit, seed, offspring, result, effect; to speak; and emotion." It refers here to the effects produced by words and emotional energy, and has another meaning of "persistence," showing that practice and repetition are important. *Hue* means "a vessel that holds water [referring to the kahuna as a receptacle for *mana*]; to move quickly [referring to the action of *mana*, which word also contains the same meaning]; to remove, expose, open, push, prod, force, wash out [all referring to the removal of complexes with the use of *mana*]." The main meanings of *hui* have to do with uniting and forming an organization, a reference to the kahuna orders. *Huo* has no meaning.

Nai means "to conquer, and to strive to obtain, endeavor to examine or understand," aims and qualities required of the kahuna. *Nae* means "shortness of breath [a lack of *mana*]; fragrant or sweet-smelling [a symbolic reference to the danger of becoming intoxicated with what one is doing]; and to parcel out equally [a call for a balanced approach]." *Nao* has to do with thrusting and probing, and an intense use of *mana* *Nau* means "to chew [with the same connotation as our digesting knowledge] and to prolong or hold the breath [a reference to a technique]."

The above is sufficient to show how much teaching can emerge from a single word in a society stressing oral traditions. From the simple word *kahuna* we can get a fairly clear picture of a highly skilled psychologist/metaphysician/healer who uses psychic abilities and life force to gain his ends, but who must also guard against the abuse of his powers. It should be easier to see now how the language itself could be used as a teaching tool.

A favorite way for the kahunas to instruct their apprentices was to present the teachings in the form of a story or legend. However, the knowledge was not in the story itself, which merely served as a vehicle, but in the names of the principle characters and locations and their interrelationships. What to Western ears might be an absurdly exaggerated tale would be, to the kahuna, a statement of philosophy or the explanation of a technique.

As an example, the legend of Moikeha, an ancient Hawaiian chief, will be cited. The following is a highly condensed version of the tale as recounted by Martha Beckwith in *Hawaiian Mythology*: "After many trials and suffering and long voyages, Moikeha arrived at the village of the popular chief Puna, fell in love with his daughter, Ho'oipo, won her hand in a contest of skill, succeeded to the chieftancy, and fathered twelve children."

To outward appearance it is no more than an exciting tale of adventure. However, in code the name *Moikeha* describes one who follows a course of action (*mo*) to master (*mo'i*) spiritual (*ha*) knowledge (*ike*) and attain great heights (*keha*) by overcoming obstacles (*ke*) and suffering (*eha*). *Puna* is also a spring or source of water (*mana*), as well as one's home, and contains meanings having to do with attaining union with one's higher self. *Ho'oipo*, the name of the chief's daughter, means "to make love or court," and contains inner meanings of succeeding in reaching or coming together with the truth in the realm of the gods. Twelve is a significant number in kahuna knowledge, and the twelve children represent the fruits of successful effort. Below the tale of adventure lies the story of a spiritual journey.

Notes

1. Max Freedom Long, *The Secret Science Behind Miracles* (Los Angeles: DeVorss & Co., 1954).

2. Ibid.

3. Lorrin Andrews, *A Dictionary of the Hawaiian Language* (Rutland, Vermont, and Tokyo: Charles E. Tuttle Co., Inc., 1974).

4. Long, *Secret Science*.

5. Roberto Assagioli, *Psychosynthesis* (New York: Viking Press, 1971).

6. Ibid.

7. Ibid.

8. Ibid.

9. William S. Kroger and William D. Fezler, *Hypnosis and Behavior Modification: Imagery Conditioning* (Philadelphia: J. B. Lippincott Co., 1976).

10. Kristin Zambucka, *Ano'Ano: The Seed* (Honolulu: Mana Publishing Co., 1978).

11. Josef Breuer and Sigmund Freud, *Studies on Hysteria*, trans. James Strachey (London: Hogarth Press and the Institute of Psychoanalysis).

12. Maxwell Maltz, *Psycho-Cybernetics* (Englewood Cliffs, N.J.: Prentice-Hall, Inc., 1960).

13. Reich, Wilhelm, *The Cancer Biopathy*, trans. Andrew White (New York: Farrar, Strauss & Giroux, 1973).

14. Ibid.

15. Maltz, *Psycho-Cybernetics.*

16. Thelma Moss, quoted in Charles Panati, *Supersenses: Our Potential for Parasensory Experience* (New York: Quadrangle/N.Y. Times Book Co., 1974).

17. Maltz, *Psycho-Cybernetics.*

18. Irving Oyle, *Time, Space & Mind* (Millbrae, CA: Celestial Arts, 1976).

19. Assagioli, *Psychosynthesis.*

20. Breuer and Freud, *Studies on Hysteria.*

21. Maltz, *Psycho-Cybernetics.*

22. Ibid.

23. Howard R. Lewis and Martha E. Lewis, *Psychosomatics* (New York: Pinnacle Books, 1975).

24. Zambucka, *Ano'Ano.*

25. Fritjof Capra, quoted in Oyle, *Time, Space & Mind.*

26. Jay Haley, *Uncommon Therapy.* New York: Ballantine Books, 1973.

27. Ibid.

28. Kroger, *Hypnosis and Behavior Modification.*

29. Reich, *Cancer Biopathy.*

30. Shared information, no reference.

31. Mary K. Pukui, E. W. Haertig, and Catherine A. Lee, *Nana I Ke Kumu* (Honolulu: Hui Hanai, 1975).

32. _____, and Samuel H. Elbert, *Hawaiian Dictionary* (Honolulu: University Press of Hawaii, 1975).

33. Oyle, *Time, Space & Mind.*

34. Assagioli, *Psychosynthesis.*

35. Kroger, *Hypnosis and Behavior Modification.*

36. Ibid.

Annotated Bibliography

This bibliography is not intended to be a comprehensive account of all the books on Huna and kahunas ever published. Instead, I have picked out books that I consider important to this study; that will allow me to expand and clarify a number of kahuna concepts; that are simply rare or interesting; and that deserve comment. I will cite only the edition I have in my library.

The Secret Science Behind Miracles, by Max Freedom Long. Los Angeles: DeVorss & Co., 1954. Max Freedom Long was a student of philosophy and psychology, with a background in Theosophy, who spent fourteen years (1917-1931) in the Hawaiian Islands as a schoolteacher and businessman. Shortly after his arrival there he became interested in the practices of the kahunas, and with the help of former Bishop Museum curator William Brigham he embarked on a lifelong study to try to discover the secrets of their knowledge. He never succeeded in getting any knowledge directly from a kahuna, though, because they were outlawed during his stay, and by the time he returned to the mainland some time later, he felt that discovering the kahuna secrets was a hopeless cause. However, his mind was still working on the problem, and in 1935 he had a sudden inspiration to examine the root words of the Hawaiian language for clues to that knowledge.

Over a period of thirty-six years he did a tremendous amount of work in decoding the language, performing experiments to test the knowledge gained, and tracing the coded knowledge in various cultures and religions around the world. He published six books, a number of pamphlets and tapes, and many volumes of a newsletter, all dealing with the study of Huna. Today his works are still the major source of public knowledge of the kahuna system, and he is frequently quoted in books on parapsychology, hypnosis and related fields.

From WK's point of view, however, although what he achieved is remarkable, Long made several errors which have led to a distorted understanding of certain points of Huna.

Quite early in *The Secret Science* Long made an assumption about the psycho-spiritual nature of man which he later treated as fact, even attributing it to a teaching of the kahunas, which it was not. While investigating the belief held in Hawaii that man has two souls (a Huna concept somewhat misunderstood in the popular Hawaiian mind), he correctly identified two descriptive words for these aspects of man—*uhane* and *unihipili*. He was also correct in connecting the first with what could be called the "conscious mind" and the second with the "subconscious." Unfortunately, he then went on to make his erroneous assumption (page 19):

> The root in *uhane* means to talk, so the spirit named in this root could talk. As only human beings talk, this spirit must be a human one. That raised the question as to the nature of the other spirit. It can grieve, and so can animals. It may not be a man who can talk, but at least it is an animal-like spirit that can grieve.

154

Based solely on this assumption, he later flatly states on page 100 that "if the kahunas are right in stating that we have in us a less-evolved lower spirit just up from the animal kingdom . . ." Both WK and Leinani Melville corroborate the existence of coded information in the Hawaiian language and its importance in understanding the Huna system, but nowhere in the kahuna teachings is there an indication that the subconscious spirit or aspect was considered less-evolved, nor that it had "graduated" (Long's term) into human form after having been an animal. Nor does Long at any point in his writings attempt to show that the code says this. He started with a guess, which he somehow began to think of as something learned through the code, and then went on to treat it as a given fact.

The second error made by Long had to do with the phenomenon of possession. Probably because of his extensive esoteric reading, Long was quite familiar with the idea that the spirits of the dead can "invade" a living person and "take over" that person's life. This, in fact, is a belief of many of the world's cultures, and was also a popular belief of the outer Hawaiian religion. With the latter belief as a support, Long concluded that this was a kahuna teaching, and made only a cursory investigation of the various words for possession and possessing spirits in the Hawaiian language. However, the kahuna code is very clear in its revelation that possession does not involve outside entities. I have shown in a Huna booklet entitled "Spirits & Possession" that possession is a process whereby hidden parts of the self are expressed as separate personalities, which may be either benign or malignant, and that nowhere in the code is there any justification for the idea that you can be taken over by something outside yourself. In this instance, the teaching of the kahunas is very close to that of most modern psychologists.

The third error has to do with the role of so-called spirits in parapsychological phenomena. In his first two books, Long placed a great deal of emphasis on this, although he agreed at the same time that most of the phenomena could be produced without recourse to such spirits. Nevertheless, he was apparently too strongly influenced by his reading and second-hand accounts in Hawaii to be able to give up the spirit idea easily. WK says—and the code shows—that anything resembling a spirit in parapsychological activity is actually a "thought-form," a condensation of etheric matter brought about through the voluntary or involuntary use of *mana* and intense imagery. This, of course, goes beyond what most modern psychologists would accept, but it is a kahuna teaching.

In all fairness, it must be allowed that Long had to contend with a number of limitations. His particular religious and esoteric background; his lack of access to a kahuna teacher and his necessary reliance on non-kahuna versions of kahuna practices; and the dictionary he had to work with, are several examples. The dictionary that Long used for his codework, for instance, was the 1865 work by Lorrin Andrews (15,000 words) which, according to Pukui and Elbert, contained many misspellings and garbled phrases. The modern student has the advantage of using the highly researched 1971 edition of the *Hawaiian Dictionary* by Mary Pukui and Samuel Elbert with 26,000 entries.

Huna: The Ancient Religion of Positive Thinking, by William R. Glover. Sunset Beach, Cal.: self-published, no date. An excellent, short book on Max Long's version of Huna, very well organized. When I say "Long's version"

I am referring to a number of ideas about Huna which Long held that were not a part of my training and/or which I cannot find justified in the kahuna code language. These include the idea that we have three separate selves evolving up from the animals, that the kahunas believed in three "grades" of *mana*, and some historical ideas about kahunas. For the most part these are differences of opinion and are relatively unimportant compared to the essence of the Huna philosophy, which is that we have the power to alter our experience. Glover does emphasize this aspect and devotes most of his book to "effective prayer" in such a positive and well-written format that I would recommend it to anyone. The use of logic to get the subconscious to change habitual beliefs is particularly well presented and is one of the most useful techniques I have ever come across. (Note: Glover misspells the Hawaiian word for *foreigner* or *whites*, giving it as *ha-oli* or *holi*, but it is actually *haole*.)

Kahuna La'au Lapa'au, by Jane Gutmanis. Norfolk Island, Australia: Island Heritage Ltd., 1977. Although this book deals exclusively with the kahuna herbal doctors of Hawaii, it contains a wealth of information on the kahuna approach to health and shows that even those who specialized in herbs enhanced their techniques with good psychology and physical manipulation, as well as telepathy, clairvoyance, colors, astrology and *mana*. While modern psychologists may question the validity of the latter, for the kahuna they are simply part of the treatment repertoire.

In her Prologue, Gutmanis describes the kahuna treatment of a woman about the year 1900. What is remarkable about the procedure is the obvious understanding on the part of the kahuna of the psychogenesis of her illness, and this was only about five years after the publication by Freud and Breuer of *Studies on Hysteria*. Also somewhat remarkable is that the woman was advised by her non-Hawaiian medical doctor to go to the kahuna, since the doctor had been unable to help her headache and constricted throat.

The kahuna began in a surprisingly modern way by first taking a "history," that is, he asked her what troubles were on her mind. She immediately related the tale of a bad quarrel with her son which had driven him from home. The pains had begun right after this. When the story was over, the kahuna ordered the family to gather certain items necessary for the healing ritual. His diagnosis was that she had done wrong and she was suffering the consequences. The pains were the result of extreme guilt, and the "gods" would have to be called on for help. First, he had the woman make a full confession of her guilt in the presence of her family. Then he performed cleansing of the house, the yard, and all their contents in order to clear the emotional atmosphere left over from the quarrel. This was in line with the kahuna belief that emotions are a form of actual energy that can affect the environment and the people who come into contact with it. Next he prepared the food and herbs, explained their symbology, consecrated them, and began to pray. Because the woman was a Christian, he first prayed to the Trinity to aid the healing. And because she was Hawaiian, he also prayed to the old Hawaiian gods. In this way he incorporated the full range of her religious beliefs. This is consistent with the idea that the treatment must always be adapted to the beliefs of the patient and that the result is more important than the method.

Once the prayers were over, the major portion of the food was given to the woman, and the rest was shared by the family. This was understood by everyone present to be a form of communion, but it was made a lighthearted and happy affair. The treatment up to this point had taken about eight hours, with the woman being the center of concerned attention. The woman was then told by the kahuna to go to sleep and that the gods would give her a dream if they were pleased with the offerings. The next morning she related a dream about her son in which all was forgiven between them. In addition her pains were all gone. However, instead of ending the treatment at that point, the kahuna went further and had the woman go through a cleansing ceremony in the sea to "seal" the cure. Part of this involved the visible placebo effect of casting a lei onto the swells to take away with it all the last vestiges of the illness. Before leaving, the kahuna directed that the woman should be given vitamin-rich sea urchins every day until she had regained her full vigor.

The resemblance to modern psychiatry in this account is so obvious that no further comment is needed. The rest of the book deals primarily with the practice of herbal medicine, but Gutmanis includes a few more accounts of treatments similar to the above.

Huna: A Beginner's Guide, by Enid Hoffman. Gloucester, Mass.: ParaResearch, 1976. A chatty, friendly book based on the teachings of Max Long, but mostly emphasizing the communication with and training of one's own subconscious. It is a very good introduction to Huna, and contains some excellent advice on how to use the pendulum for self-awareness and self-development. Hoffman correctly notes that Long originated the use of the pendulum in connection with the Huna concept of subconscious communication and training.

Imagineering for Health, by Serge King. Wheaton, Ill.:

Theosophical Publishing House, Quest Books, 1981. This book by me doesn't contain a single Hawaiian word nor any mention of kahunas, but it is based entirely on my Huna training and study. Part I deals with the nature of beliefs and the mind; Part II relates beliefs and illness to particular areas of the body; and Part III is full of practical healing techniques.

The Kahuna: Versatile Mystics of Old Hawaii, by L. R. McBride. Hilo, Hawaii: Petroglyph Press, 1972. This is an excellent little book by a man who obviously has a deep love and respect for things Hawaiian. In the second chapter he tells of legends regarding white priests or kahunas who were brought from foreign lands, and he quotes a historical source to the effect that "two of the most prominent high priests in all the islands were among the descendants of these foreigners." There is considerable information on the various kinds of kahuna experts, including healers, and a very good chapter on the power of words. Throughout the book there are many Hawaiian words and phrases that would be of interest to anyone wanting to do more research on Huna.

Children of the Rainbow, by Leinani Melville. Wheaton, Ill.: Theosophical Publishing House, Quest Books, 1969. Melville was given the task of writing this book on the religion, legends and gods of pre-Christian Hawaii by his grandmother in the early 1930s. However, he didn't finish it until the late sixties. He says he was helped by Lahilahi Webb, a former custodian of Hawaiiana at the Bishop Museum in Honolulu, who showed him how to decode the Hawaiian language. He also got help from an unnamed elderly Hawaiian lady who taught him the spiritual truths he writes about. Melville insists on using the Tahitian pronunciation for Hawaiian words, saying at one point that "The missionaries, after establishing a foothold, concocted a new language for the 'heathen they had come to save from the pit of darkness,' to use one of their own expressions. They removed the native *R* and replaced it with an *L*, changed the *T* to a *K*, and substituted *W* for *V*." This is linguistic nonsense, but Melville is obviously not well disposed toward the missionaries. He relates a number of legends as he must have heard them and indulges in some highly creative translations of the *Kumulipo* verses. The Polynesians are traced back to Mu, which he also calls *Ta Rua*, and kahuna teachings are presented in a very "spiritual" style. About a third of the book is taken up by old Hawaiian symbols used on cloth and elsewhere. The symbols are valid, but Melville's interpretation of their meaning is open to question.

The Kahunas: The Black—and White—Magicians of Hawaii, edited by Sibley S. Morrill. Boston: Branden Press, 1969. A collection of ten short articles on kahunas by nineteenth and twentieth century authors, this small book contains interesting historical material and viewpoints. In one article Morrill says:

> Indeed, if we make just a reasonable attempt to judge the matter on the evidence offered, the only sensible thing for us to do is at least to make a serious study of Hawaiian kahuna claims—not for the purpose of disproving them, but merely for finding out what the facts are, a procedure that should be adopted in the examination of any subject of interest and dispute.

J. S. Emerson, whose Christian prejudice shows in his reference to "the unspeakable abominations of *hula*," nevertheless demonstrates good insight when he says in relation to a kahuna ceremony, "In short, the god does not make the kahuna, but the kahuna often makes his god." Francis J. Green wrote about the training of Maori *tohungas* (kahunas) and said that at the end of a five-year course the candidate had to pass four tests, the last of which was to bewitch a slave or captive and make him fall down dead. Since these were not renegades, I believe it more likely that this last test has to do with hypnosis and causing unconsciousness with a large charge of *mana*, rather than death.

The Miracle of Mana-Force, by Madeleine C. Morris. West Nyack, N.Y.: Parker Publishing Co., 1975. There is a certain class of books that I call "pop-positive." They have snappy titles, techniques with pseudo-technological names, and they promise you wealth, love and power beyond your wildest dreams. Sometimes, in spite of the hyperbole, they still contain good information. Morris's book is one of these. The chapter titles are enough to turn off many serious students of Huna (examples: "Mana-Force Fieldomics; Pushing the Magic MFP Button for Any Amount of Money; Mana-Force Charmetrics"), and the "case histories" get very tiresome. Nevertheless, the book is actually full of well-organized, workable techniques for very specific situations. As such, it fills a need that most other books on Huna do not satisfy. Unfortunately, Morris claims that she got all this knowledge about *mana*, the three selves and *aka* directly from a kahuna, when it is painfully obvious from her phraseology that she lifted it right from Max Long without giving him any credit.

Nana I Ke Kumu, by Mary K. Pukui, E. W. Haertig, and Catherine A. Lee. Honolulu: Hui Hanai, 1975. A unique work, *Nana I Ke Kumu* (*Look to the Source*) was published by the Queen Liliuokalani Children's Center, a child welfare center, for the purpose of presenting and clarifying Hawaiian cultural concepts and comparing them to modern psychiatric and psychological understandings. As the authors state, it was intended primarily for physicians, psychiatrists, nurses, psychologists, social workers, clergy, etc., who work with Hawaiians. Many cultural misunderstandings have occurred between Hawaiians in need and non-Hawaiians in the helping professions, and these have greatly hindered the giving of effective assistance. In format, the book presents Hawaiian words or phrases representing deeply held concepts and then explains them by case histories and analysis. Most of the explanations were obtained from Mary Pukui, whose Hawaiian ancestors include kahunas. As a result, many traditional kahuna concepts and practices are included, as well as references to mystic and psychic experiences. In the words of the authors:

> There are many references to supernatural or mystic occurrences. Though psychiatric parallels or interpretations, necessary to the purpose of this book are often given, the authors do not consider it their prerogative either to agree or disagree with the preternatural character of the incidents. These mystic experiences have been reported as accurately as possible. Their inclusion in this volume is essential. Hawaiian life and thought cannot be understood without knowing about them.

Throughout the book, the authors repeatedly point out how many modern Hawaiians have garbled the ancient knowledge and no longer understand their own traditions as taught by the kahunas of old. This often results in psychogenic disorders based on faulty beliefs of such a nature that non-Hawaiians cannot relate to them.

The authors additionally mention that experiences such as seeing and talking with visions, which a modern psychiatrist might classify as schizophrenic, are not necessarily pathological in the Hawaiian context.

Among the many insights offered by this book, one that stands out in terms of the present work is the explanation of the *ho'oponopono* concept. This is a form of family/group therapy practiced from ancient times up to the present day, usually led by a kahuna or senior member of the family. Its resemblance to modern group therapy is striking. The basic format, taken from the book, is as follows:

Opening prayer and prayers any time they seem necessary.

A statement of the obvious problem to be solved or prevented from growing worse.

The "setting to rights" of each successive problem that becomes apparent (called *mahiki*, "peeling away").

Self-scrutiny and discussion of individual conduct, attitudes and emotions.

A quality of absolute truthfulness and sincerity.

Control of disruptive emotions by channeling discussion through the leader.

Questioning of involved participants by the leader.

Honest confession to the gods (or God) and to each other of wrongdoing, grievances, grudges and resentments.

Immediate restitution or arrangements to make restitution as soon as possible.

Mutual forgiveness and releasing from guilts, grudges
and tensions occasioned by the wrongdoing.

Closing prayer (and ritual).

After the settlement of a dispute, the leader would
declare *ho'omalu* (peace), indicating that the subject
was closed for good and should not be brought up again.
A second volume of *Nana I Ke Kumu* has very good
chapters on kahunas and healing, dreams, ESP and self-
image concepts among Hawaiians.

The Kahuna Sorcerers of Hawaii, Past and Present, by
Julius Scammon Rodman. Hicksville, N.Y.: Exposition
Press, 1979. This book is very interesting and informative
from many points of view, the least of which has to do
with real kahuna knowledge. In that respect it is primarily a collection of superstitions about kahunas, and
while Rodman gives lip service to kahuna healers, he
seems more interested in terrifying the reader with tales
of kahuna curses. The tone of the book is set in the
preface by Evelyn Wells, who says of kahunas that:

> If you meet with one, seated beside you perhaps at a
> lunch counter or bar, he will seem to be an ordinary
> person, but you must do or say nothing to offend
> him. You will recognize him by the ruby flash when
> he focuses on you. His eyes have been turned a flaming
> red by the magic potions that have helped develop
> his extraordinary powers.

This description is so picturesque that a popular TV show
that takes place in Hawaii used it as the basis for a
program involving a kahuna, complete with special
effects. Actually, the superstition about a red-eyed
kahuna (*kahuna makole*) stems from the fact that *makole*
is a play on words, which is a favorite Hawaiian enter-

tainment. It is a contraction of *maka ole*, a euphemism of *maka ula*, which also means "red-eyed," but which means as well "prophet or magician" when said as one word, *makaula*. And kahunas do not get their "extraordinary powers" from magic potions but from mental disciplines. Besides making full use of superstitious tales, Rodman employs innuendo whenever there are no sources to back up his ideas. For instance, he says, "There is no way of knowing at this late date the extent of Chinese influences upon certain Hawaiian kahuna practices." He then goes on to assume they did have influence by the mere fact of their presence ("A Chinese was manufacturing sugar in 1802"). His inconsistency is rampant as well. After acknowledging Mary K. Pukui as the "leading Hawaiian authority in matters of classical culture," he virtually says her statements about pre-discovery kahuna practices are not to be trusted. To Rodman's credit, he includes in his work some highly interesting letters and manuscript material from Leinani Melville; critical commentary by Charles Kenn, noted authority on Hawaiiana and one of the few teachers of the art of *lua* (hand-to-hand combat); and good historical photographs. About a third of his book is given over to ancient and modern burial practices and his search for Kamehameha's treasure, none of which has anything to do with kahunas, even though it is interesting.

Ano'Ano: The Seed, by Kristin Zambucka. Honolulu: Mana Publishing Co., 1978. A short book written in quasi-poetic style with beautiful illustrations, it is full of kahuna teachings in condensed form. The teachings are presented as a story in which islanders are seeking the truth about themselves and their world. Zambucka says she completed it "after numerous years of researching and painting in the Pacific area." WK recommends it as a good illustration of kahuna ideas. Among the ideas presented is this one, which is a fundamental premise of the kahuna psychosomatic healing approach and very appropriate as a conclusion to this volume:

> Though I may travel far I will meet only what I carry with me for every man is a mirror. We see only ourselves reflected in those around us. Their attitudes and actions are reflections of our own. The whole world and its conditions has its counterpart within us all. Turn the gaze inward. Correct yourself and your world will change.

Further References

Assagioli, Roberto. *The Act of Will*. Baltimore: Penguin Books, Inc., 1974.

Beckwith, Martha. *The Kumulipo*. Honolulu: University Press of Hawaii, 1972.

Benson, Herbert. *The Relaxation Response*. New York: William Morrow & Co., Inc., 1975.

Buck, Peter H. *Vikings of the Pacific*. Chicago: University of Chicago Press, 1972.

Churchward, James. *The Children of Mu*. New York: Ives Washburn, 1956.

Ellis, William. *Polynesian Researches: Hawaii*. Tokyo: Charles E. Tuttle Co., 1969.

Feher, Joseph, ed. *Hawaii: A Pictorial History*. Honolulu: Bishop Museum Press, 1969.

Fornander, Abraham. *An Account of the Polynesian Race*. Tokyo: Charles E. Tuttle Co., 1969.

Heyerdahl, Thor. *Aku-Aku*. New York: Allen and Unwin, 1958.

Kalakaua, David. *The Legends and Myths of Hawaii*. Tokyo: Charles E. Tuttle Co., 1972.

King, Serge V. *The Hidden Knowledge of Huna Science*. Santa Monica: Huna Enterprises, 1976.

Long, Max Freedom. *Growing Into Light*. Los Angeles: De Vorss, 1955.

_____. *The Huna Code in Religions*. Los Angeles: De Vorss, 1965.

———. *Psychometric Analysis*. Los Angeles: De Vorss, 1959.

———. *The Secret Science at Work*. Los Angeles: Huna Research Publications, 1953.

———. *Self-Suggestion and the New Huna Theory of Mesmerism and Hypnosis*. Los Angeles: De Vorss, 1958.

Miller, Hyman, and Dorothy W. Baruch. *The Practice of Psychosomatic Medicine*. New York: McGraw-Hill, 1956.

Nau, Erika. *Self Awareness Through Huna*. Virginia Beach: Donning, 1981.

Pukui, Mary K., and Caroline Curtis. *Tales of the Mene-hune*. Honolulu: Kamehameha Schools Press, 1971.

Steiger, Brad. *Secrets of Kahuna Magic*. New York: Award Books, 1971.

Straith-Miller, Elizabeth. *Huna: An Introduction to Its Teachings*. (Rare), Church of St. Michael.

Index

Index

Diet, 115-17. *See also* Foods; Weight, control of

Ecological feedback, 105-8
Emotionals, 11-12. *See also Ku*, Order of
Emotions, 56, 86, 93-96
Energy flow, biological, 91-93. *See also Mana*; Orgone energy
Erickson, Milton, 110
Europeans in Hawaii, 25-28. *See also Lono*, Captain Cook as

Failure, treatment, 129-32
Fasting, Kahuna view of, 117
Fears and guilts, 75-76
Foods: *mana* in, 63, 91-92, 116; reflect mental state, 115. *See also* Diet
Freud, Sigmund, 83, 98, 127; psychosomatic approach of, 86, 100, 106, 110

God, 40-42, 45-46, 57, 132-33; paths to, 138; personal (*see* God-self)
God-self, 45, 46, 83-85, 88. *See also* healing, divine approach; Higher Self; *Kane*
Gods (*akua*). *See Kanaloa, Kane, Ku, Lono*
Graf, Bernard, 115
Group therapy, 118

Habit, 88-89, 125-26
Haley, Jay, 110-11

Healing, 33-34, 56-58, 71-72, 95; divine approach, 132-33; effect on healer of, 123-24; energy approach, 120-24; "faith," 131; god of (*see Kanaloa*); Kahuna methods of, 109-33 *passim*; material approach, 111-20; mental approach, 124-29; traditional African, 7. *See also* Aromatherapy; Beliefs; Body, physical; Complexes, belief; Diet; Ecological feedback; Emotions; Foods; Hypnosis; Illness; Imagination; *Mana*; Tension, release of; Therapeutic touch
Heinlein, Robert, 133
Heyerdahl, Thor, 20
Higher Self, 81-85, 89, 98, 131. *See also* God-self; Healing, divine approach; *Kane*
Hula, 121
Huna, defined, 8
Huna International, Order of, 8
Hypnosis, 96, 110, 118, 127

Illness, 91, 106-8, 113; stress related to, 104-5. *See also* Healing
Imagination, 62, 63, 126; creative (*laulele*), 87, 128; guided (*makaku*) 125, 128
Intellectuals, 11-12. *See also Lono*, Order of
Intuitionists, 11-12, 14, 15. *See also Kane*, Order of

Jung, Carl, 87

171

Index

QUEST BOOKS

are published by
The Theosophical Society in America,
a branch of a world organization
dedicated to the promotion of brotherhood and
the encouragement of the study of religion,
philosophy, and science, to the end that man may
better understand himself and his place in
the universe. The Society stands for complete
freedom of individual search and belief.
In the Theosophical Classics Series
well-known occult works are made
available in popular editions.

More "self-help" books published by Quest

Art of Inner Listening—*By Jessie Crum*
"So you would like to be a genius," writes the author. Simply stop talking—and listen—really listen.

Concentration—*By Ernest Wood*
Will help you take full charge of your mind.

Do You See What I See?—*By Jae Jah Noh*
How to live fully, indeed passionately, with no inner conflicts.

Imagineering for Health—*By Serge King*
Self-healing through use of the mind

Mastering the Problems of Living—*By Haridas Chaudhuri*
Overcome depression! Conquer anxiety! Make decisions!

The Path of Healing—*By H. K. Challoner*
Based on the holistic nature of all life. Heal yourself with harmonious living.

A Way to Self-Discovery—*By I. K. Taimni*
A way of life book for serious students of the "ancient wisdom."

**Available from:
The Theosophical Publishing House
306 West Geneva Road, Wheaton, Illinois 60187**

Serge King
5072 Kamamalu Lp.
Kauai
826-9097